Parma: Notes from a Year in Serie A

Greg Burke was born in St Louis, Missouri, and played pretty decent full-back in a short career at St Gabriel the Archangel elementary school. He has lived in Rome for ten years and works as a correspondent for *Time* magazine.

PARMA

Notes from a Year in Serie A

GREG BURKE

VICTOR GOLLANCZ

LONDON

First published in Great Britain 1998
by Victor Gollancz
An imprint of the Cassell Group
Wellington House, 125 Strand, London WC2R 0BB

A Gollancz Paperback Original

A catalogue record for this book is
available from the British Library.

ISBN 0 575 06642 3

Typeset by Rowland Phototypesetting Ltd,
Bury St Edmunds, Suffolk
Printed and bound in Guernsey by
Guernsey Press Co. Ltd, Channel Isles

98 99   5 4 3 2 1

With the collaboration of Antonio Saccone, who stuck close to Ancelotti for the entire match.

Acknowledgements

I'd like to thank Giorgio Bottaro of Parma Calcio and Ian Preece at Victor Gollancz. Without them this book would have never been written. Thanks also to those who either encouraged or put up with this bit of temporary madness: Megan Rise, for her calm in keeping order in all my papers and files; Francesco De Leonardis and the rest of the Ripa Boys, Gabriel Kahn, Paolo Melis, Benedicta Cipolla, Jean-Marie Guenois and Blandine Becharas. A few people who actually know something about football were also helpful, especially Andrea Schianchi and Lanfranco Vaccari at *La Gazzetta dello Sport*, Emilio Marrese and Valentina Desalvo at *La Repubblica*, Pino Cobribi and Marco Trabucchi. Christopher Winner did double duty as coach and sportsfan.

Contents

Contents

Introduction

I sometimes believe I'm the most objective football fan in all of Italy. Although I love the sport, I don't have a team. For certain periods of time I have been closer to one squad or another, depending on various irrational choices. On arriving in Italy ten years ago I immediately identified with the great German midfielder Lothar Matthäus, then playing with Internazionale. I have a lot of German blood, and look a little like Matthäus. Inter were having one of their best seasons ever, and I kept my eye on my alter ego.

Then Inter faded and Lothar left Italy and I was left without a team. I was trying to learn French at the time, so I started to follow Paris Saint-Germain from the pages of *Le Figaro*. I live in Rome, and among the hometown squads, I found Lazio slightly more appealing than Roma, but not for any particularly sophisticated reasons. Lazio wear sky-blue jerseys, and that's a colour I like. Roma colours are red and yellow, neither of them my favourites.

While I didn't write on sports frequently, I did occasional interviews with footballers. And this would usually lead me to rooting for them in a certain way. So after a long, leisurely Saturday afternoon interview with David Platt, I watched him and Bari drop into the second division. Bari stayed; Platt was rescued by Juventus. Or was it Sampdoria? Then a two-minute post-match chat with Milan striker George Weah made me something of a *Milanista*, or at least a Weahista, since neither of the most successful Italian teams in recent decades, Milan or Juventus, has ever attracted me very much. I don't like Juve's jerseys (the zebra stripes make the players look too much like American referees) and I don't care for Milan's obnoxious fans. But Weah was one worth watching, and he won FIFA's Player of the Year award in his first season at Milan.

Platt and Weah both won me over. I wished them well, and continue to do so. But when I interviewed Paul Gascoigne, who was briefly at Lazio, my feelings were just the opposite. Occasionally brilliant on the field, he was invariably making a fool of himself elsewhere, getting in bar brawls and punching out photographers. Gazza was one reason not to root for Lazio, nice jerseys or not.

I can proudly say that, unlike Nick Hornby, I am not someone who can think of nothing but football and spends great periods of each day like a total moron. No squad has gotten me in that can't-think-about-anything-else-but mode, and that's probably all for the best. At least it allows me to get some work done and pay the bills.

While I don't have a team in the first division, I do have a national team, and follow it with attention. As a US citizen, logic and loyalty would put me with the Americans (guys with very unWASPish names like Rodriguez, Meola and Vinceguerra) but that would be like trying to root for the Italian national baseball team (maybe next century, guys). And yet, I wouldn't have jumped out the window if Italy had not qualified for the World Cup in France. I may not sleep well if the Italian squad plays poorly, but I'll sleep. If Roberto Baggio muffs a shot in front of an open goal, that's his problem, not mine. He's the guy who should have problems sleeping.

But I do love the sport, and I live in the right place for it. Italy offers a better array of stars than any other country in the world. In the last ten years I've seen Lothar Matthäus, Diego Maradona, George Weah, Paulo Sousa, Lilian Thuram, and now Ronaldo. There was also the Dutch trio of Frank Rikaard, Ruud Gullit and Marco Van Basten, all in the same Milan squad. And Gascoigne, of course, who came to entertain us in Rome for a year. But, ultimately, New York has Broadway, while Italy has football.

The idea for this book came on a lazy May day when I sent faxes to three coaches whom I consider winners. I didn't think any of them would respond and I might have let it all drop right there and written a book on Italian fashion instead. Football is one of the few things that works well in this country, and fashion is another one.

This was in the spring of 1997. Marcello Lippi of Juventus was busy on two fronts: winning the Serie A title and preparing for the Final of the Champions League with Borussia Dortmund (which he would unexpectedly lose 3–1). Fabio Capello was at Real Madrid but fighting with management there and on his way back to a delicate situation at Milan, who had just gone through two coaches and were about to finish closer to the bottom than the top of the pack of eighteen teams. Carlo Ancelotti was at Parma, fighting for 2nd place and a berth in the Champions League.

I'd be curious to know where my faxes to Lippi and Capello ended up. Probably in the same pile that 1000 other requests for interviews were being stashed. Fortunately Giorgio Bottaro at Parma read the fax for Ancelotti and a woman from his office gave me a call to set up an appointment. Bottaro wears two hats at Parma. He's head of the press office, and also 'team manager', which means he organizes everything from what the players will wear when they go on the road, to what hotel they'll be staying in, to what friendly matches they'll play before and after the season. Bottaro, 38, came to Parma in 1996 after working as head of player personnel for a volleyball team in Ravenna, on the Adriatic coast.

My assistant, Antonio Saccone, is a great driver, and we battled the rain for five hours from Rome to Parma, via Florence and Bologna. We almost missed the appointment, actually. We first went to Parma's baseball stadium rather than Tardini, the football grounds, but we eventually found the right place. The first encounter with Ancelotti didn't last more than thirty minutes, since the squad were leaving for a post-season friendly, but it was a good start. Ancelotti told us to come back in July when the team would be on retreat in the Alps, and we took him up on his offer.

The rest you can read about in the following pages. I had never been a Parma fan, but a colleague who covered sports for Reuters,

Jeff Donovan, was always telling me about them, and we went to see them against Lazio once, so I did know who Gianfranco Zola and Dino Baggio were, as well as Ancelotti. Of course Zola had already gone off to England and been replaced by another tiny but inventive striker, Enrico Chiesa. At the Lazio match, I remember being struck by the talent of Lilian Thuram and Fabio Cannavaro, two of the best defenders in the game today. As I was walking home with Jeff after the match, Cannavaro pulled alongside in his BMW and asked how to get to the highway for Naples. He was going to spend his day off in his hometown.

When I got started on this project I really didn't care if Parma won the *scudetto* (league championship) or not. It's not a book solely about Parma or about Ancelotti. It's about the eighteen teams in Serie A, and the battle for the *scudetto*. I've tried to explain the Italian top division from the perspective of Parma and their manager. Of course, the fact that the team is competitive and the manager is a decent guy with twenty years of experience (he was one of the best midfielders in Serie A in the 1980s) helped immensely.

When I first approached Ancelotti about this project, I was awfully ambitious. I wanted to hound him for an entire season, sitting in on every dressing-room talk with his players and every huddle with his coaches. He told me I was crazy, but we kept talking. Not even the president of the team, who forked out 18 billion lire (more than £6 million) for Enrico Chiesa, gets in the dressing room. Ancelotti named another prominent and highly successful Italian coach. You know how long it would take him to tell you to go to hell? he asked. 'Three seconds. One, two, three. Go to hell.' Ancelotti never told me nor my assistant Antonio to get lost during the twelve months we talked, although he was probably tempted to at times. He patiently walked us through the ups and downs of a season in Serie A, and it was a great hike.

Glossary: A Few Useful Italian Terms

Arbitro: referee
Azzurri: 'the Blues' or the Italian national team
Biancocelesti: white and blues, or *Laziali*
Bianconeri: white and blacks, or *Juventini*
Calcio: football
Catenaccio: dirty chain, a fall-back defence
Campionato: the championship
Capocannoniere: top scorer
Curva: the curve, the cheap seats at each end of a stadium
Fantasista: the fantasy man, or playmaker
Gialloblu: yellow and blues, or Parma supporters
Giallorossi: yellow and reds, *Romanisti*
Mezzaclassifica: mid-table
Mezzapunta: half-striker, plays between midfield and attack
Mister: manager
Nerazzurri: black and blues, *Interisti*
Regista: field commander
Rossoneri: red and blacks, or Milan players and supporters
Scudetto: the 'little shield' or league championship
Serie A: the top division in Italian professional football, followed by Serie B, C1 and C2
Scugnizzo: Naples street kid, shrewd and amusing
Silenzio stampa: refusal to speak to the media
Spettacolo: action or excitement
Straniero: foreigner
Tifoso: supporter
Trascinatore: the game-maker, or natural team leader
Tribuna: the best seats, in the grandstand

Ultras: Rabid, organized fans, the closest Italy comes to hooligans
Viola: Fiorentina, on account of their violet jerseys

1 They Call Him Mister

On May 17 1992, Carlo Ancelotti was sitting on the bench of AC Milan, and steaming. He wanted to be on the pitch. Milan had already clinched their twelfth Serie A title, and this was Ancelotti's last game as a professional football player. The Devils, who had not lost all season, were winning again. The fans, aware that 'Carletto' would be leaving them, began chanting his name. Manager Fabio Capello, never one to be accused of an excess of sentimentality, must have heard the cheering. He finally called for Ancelotti to enter the game, against Verona, with 20 minutes left. Despite the limited amount of time he had to work with, Ancelotti could not have scripted a better farewell. He scored two goals, something he had never done in nearly 300 games in Serie A.

The final score was Milan 4 Verona 0. It certainly wasn't the most important match for Milan, or Ancelotti, but it showed the character of the 32-year-old midfielder. He came into a difficult situation, having just 20 minutes to settle, and made the best of it. Two goals. Ancelotti has frequently shown what he's got, inside and out. As a player, he came back twice from torn ligaments, in both knees. And in two years of coaching he has twice bounced back from terrible starts.

The two goals against Verona were not the only goals scored during his thirteen-year career, of course. Ancelotti, who still has a powerful shot and occasionally works out with his keepers at the end of training, scored the first goal in Milan's 5–0 rout of Real Madrid in the 1989 European Cup (now called Champions League) Final, a booming shot from outside the penalty area. He also resolved a few other matches with key goals. But essentially Ancelotti was more of a defensive-minded midfielder, what's known as an *incontrista* in Italy, somebody who's there to create problems for the opposing team and keep them from bringing the ball upfield.

Although he began his professional career in Serie C at Parma in 1976, at the age of 17, he went to Serie A and Roma in 1979, and played for their championship team in 1983. He was then bought by Milan, and he won two *scudetti* and eight cups while with Silvio Berlusconi's powerhouse squad. Ancelotti was also on the national team from 1981 to 1992. A scouting report on Ancelotti would have read something like: 'Midfielder. Very solid. Combative but clean. Not brilliant offensively but shoots well from a distance. Good character. Generous. Uses his head.'

Ancelotti, who had suffered the knee injuries in 1982 and 1983, both of which required major surgery, wisely didn't try to stretch his career further than he should. But that meant he was already finishing up when he had just turned 33. That's an age when most Italian mamma's-boys-turned-professionals – doctors and lawyers, for example – are just getting started.

AC Milan, owned by the media magnate Berlusconi, and one of Italy's wealthiest and most ambitious clubs, made an offer to Ancelotti to stay with the organization and work with their youngsters. But Ancelotti had an even better opportunity. Arrigo Sacchi, manager of the national team, had promised Carlo that he would bring him on as his assistant. Sacchi, a former Milan skipper, kept his promise, and Carlo found himself training the midfield of a team that would go to the finals of the 1994 World Cup in Los Angeles – but not without difficulties. They lost to Ireland in their opening game, drew with Mexico, and had to come from behind to beat Nigeria to make it to the quarter-finals.

They eventually got their act together, beat Spain and Bulgaria, and made it to the Final against Brazil. And Ancelotti was not embarrassed by Italy's loss to Brazil. 'You've got to remember that even though Italy made it to the Final in 1970, we lost 4–1 that time,' he says. 'But in the States we lost on penalty kicks.'

In Italy it's an unwritten rule that if you don't win it all, you resign. Sacchi, who was violently attacked for his style of play –

and his obsessive attachment to schemes – didn't resign, exactly, but he got an offer from Milan, and took it. For Sacchi, it was a return to Milan, but not the same squad he had left five years earlier. They were in trouble.

Sacchi took over from the Uruguayan Oscar Washington Tabarez twelve games into the 1996–97 season, and after they finished in 11th place, the manager's contract wasn't renewed. (Ancelotti, in his first year at Parma, beat Milan and his mentor Sacchi at San Siro 1–0 just before Christmas.) Sacchi had other offers but refused them, took a year off and hung low. Although he was occasionally seen at some important games, he didn't give any interviews. Essentially he disappeared from Italian football for a year.

As national coach, Sacchi provoked more intense feelings of love and hate than almost anyone else in the game. He was called a fanatic and the Stalin of Italian football, always ready for a purge. One of the sports dailies relentlessly attacked him for seventeen consecutive days. But he changed the style of play in Serie A, making it a much faster game. Sacchi was not the first coach to play a zone defence but he was the first to play an 'offside defence', getting rid of the old 'libero', or stopper, and playing four defenders in line. It was a real change in mentality, and probably only worked because of the level of the guys he had playing for him: national team defenders such as Franco Baresi, Paolo Maldini, Alessandro Costacurta and Marco Tassotti. The defenders had to be attentive to the fact they were in line; if one fell back the system would break down.

Sacchi also purged Italians of their fear of playing away. For decades Italian squads were content with a draw when they weren't at home. Italian sides also liked to score a goal or two, and then hunker down. Not Sacchi, his squads played to win, and win big. In his four seasons at Milan between 1987 and 1991, the club always managed to finish among the top three.

Players were always expected to be on the move, and Sacchi brought a whole new intensity to training sessions. 'Sacchi always had this look in his eyes – even in a friendly match – like he was about to have an apparition from the Virgin Mary,' complains

Lanfranco Vaccari, deputy editor at *La Gazzetta dello Sport*. 'That,' counters Ancelotti, 'is Sacchi's strength.' One man's fanaticism is another's rigour and discipline.

Sacchi broke with Milan in 1991 because he couldn't get along with their star striker, Marco Van Basten, and the high-scoring Dutchman meant more to the team than the coach. Ancelotti has always been a Sacchi man, and speaks with him frequently. 'I don't think he has a lot of desire to coach again, at least in Italy,' Ancelotti said. 'Football can give you incredible satisfaction, but I guarantee that the disappointments are also terribly intense. It might be fear of those kind of disappointments that keeps Sacchi from coming back.'

Sacchi eventually did come back, but not in Italy. After talks with both Paris Saint-Germain and Atlético Madrid, he finally signed a two-year contract – worth an estimated $2 million a year – with Atlético. Sacchi has also hedged his bet with the Spanish club, and in the event that he's let go before the contract is up, he'll receive an enormous golden parachute.

Sacchi and Ancelotti have a tremendous amount of respect and admiration for each other. When Sacchi went to Milan in 1987, he insisted that the squad buy Ancelotti from Roma. 'At Milan there was some resistance about getting Ancelotti,' recalled Sacchi. 'One doctor told me that we were taking a player who had lost 20 to 30 per cent of his ability on account of injuries. I told him I could deal with that as long as he had 100 per cent character and motivation. And he turned out to be one of the cornerstones of that Milan side.'

Sacchi didn't know Ancelotti personally before bringing him to Milan, but he had formed an opinion by watching him play. They had some friends in common and Milan's new 'Mister', as managers are called in Italy, talked with them. He liked what he heard. Dependable. Generous. Humble. Wants to improve. Very determined. 'The injuries reduced his ability, but strengthened his character,' Sacchi said. 'He recovered from the injuries thanks to a real strong will.' Perhaps what Sacchi liked best about Ancelotti was his down-to-earth attitude, a good head on very solid shoulders: 'He's not a prima donna.'

Sacchi admittedly recruited Roma's midfielder more for his temperament than for his skill, although he said the skill was tremendous and that he considered him a 'complete' player. 'He's got the right character and the right personality,' Sacchi noted. 'He's somebody who's got values.' Was Ancelotti favoured at the start of his management career by an extra dose of fortune? Sacchi doesn't think so. 'Good luck is what the others call your ability,' he snorted. 'Fortune falls on those who are ready to grab it.'

Ancelotti finally got his chance as a head coach in 1995, but the job nearly ended just two months after it began. He had been called by Reggiana, who were in Serie B and close to his home-town of Reggiolo, not far from Bologna in central Italy. After the squad was still without a victory and in last place after seven games, the Mister thought he would resign. But there were two things that kept him from calling it quits. 'One, that's the first thing they teach you at coaching school – never resign,' he recalled. 'And then my wife told me not to bag it. And I trust her opinion.'

But there were moments when he thought he would give up football and return to his roots, producing wine. He could also keep busy investing the money he made while playing professional football, most of it at the top level, for nearly two decades. But he started winning, and Reggiana finished the season in 3rd place, which meant they were to be promoted to Serie A. Ancelotti was either a good coach, a lucky coach, or a miracle worker. And he was suddenly a very sought after young man.

Carletto (Little Carlo) also won his own promotion, when Parma came knocking on his door. It was like going home for Ancelotti, who, of course, had begun his career at Parma, then in Serie C, when he was still a teenager. At Parma Calcio headquarters today there's a poster-size photo of a very young Ancelotti as he brings the ball downfield in the old Parma jersey – a black cross on a white background. The coach at the time was Cesare Maldini, later to become head of the Italian national team.

In thirteen years in Serie A, Carlo Ancelotti never had any chronic health problems. Torn ligaments in both knees, yes, but nothing recurrent. Once he started running a team in Serie A, however, he discovered that every Sunday he was suffering from gastritis. 'Managing is a lot more difficult,' he said. 'I was a lot more serene as a player; I'd go into the games with a lot less tension. Now that's impossible. All the pressure and all the responsibility seem to concentrate on one person, and that's me.'

Ancelotti tries not to show his emotion too much during the matches, preferring to lean against the plastic protection covering the bench. He remains almost motionless. Until, of course, Parma score, at which point he takes a few steps, jumps and punches his fist in the air with joy. If Parma concede a goal, his 92 kilos remain stationary, or sometimes he puts his hands in his hair if the mistakes that led to the score were especially bad.

While Ancelotti saw his share of success in his career as a midfielder, he also proved himself early on as a coach. After the success at Reggiana, Ancelotti worked his second miracle in two years, bringing Parma, a squad that had only been in Serie A since 1990, to the second spot in the standings. He gained a reputation as a tough, defensive-minded coach. Perhaps Parma would not score a lot of goals, but they would give up even fewer. Since the Champions League expanded to take both the winners and the runners-up of every league, the new coach had won a place for Parma in that tournament. Champions League translated into prestige and money for the club.

Although most of the coaches in Serie A are former players, few have the long first division experience of Ancelotti. And yet the Mister doesn't believe good players necessarily make good coaches. 'Your experience as a player isn't really a lot of help as a coach,' he says. 'It can help you somewhat in understanding the players better.' He predicted that Gianluca Vialli, player-coach at Chelsea, would only have success if he separates the two roles. 'If he puts aside his experience as a player I think he'll do fine, because he's somebody with a lot of charisma and a lot of personality.' This, of course was before Chelsea beat Stuttgart in the Cup Winners' Cup, Vialli calling in Zola off the bench to witness his fellow Italian scoring less than a minute later. Italian managers' stock rose once again. Vialli's success could have never happened in Italy. For one, player-managers are frowned upon as being unprofessional, and, secondly, a new manager in Italy would start out in Serie B or C, not in the equivalent of the Premier League.

Ancelotti's passion for running a squad in Serie A is almost identical to his passion for playing. He likes showing that he's got the right stuff, that at least occasionally he and his boys can go out and beat the best teams in football. And so he was satisfied after a 2–2 draw with Juventus early in the season, even though Parma were twice in the lead and should have won the game. 'We played head to head with the best team in the world,' he stated, flatly. 'I can't complain about that.'

There's loads of pressure but also plenty of money for a mister in Serie A. Salaries at the bigger squads will make a manager a billionaire, at least in lire, and quite possibly a millionaire in dollars. Nevertheless, Carletto has promised himself that he will pull out of coaching after a few years. He's convinced he doesn't have the stamina of someone like Giovanni Trapattoni, currently with Bayern Munich, formerly of Inter and Juventus, who's been on the bench for more than 500 first division games.

The problems that come with coaching are the stress – not to mention gastritis – and the lack of time. 'I've got a lot less time for my family than when I was a player,' Ancelotti complains. 'Sure, there were always retreats, and there are now, too. But now the problem is unplugging from football when you're home with your wife. I just can't do it.'

Ancelotti lives a in two-storey stone house about fifteen minutes' drive outside of Parma, on a hill overlooking several vineyards. The Mister has been married since 1983 to Luisa Ghibellini, who serves as his manager. 'She's very tight with money,' Carlo said, with a smile. Ancelotti despises agents, and doesn't hide his feelings. 'Their role is to safeguard the interests of the player,' he notes. 'But the interests of the player aren't always the same as the interests of the team. So a player who has problems with his team or with his manager doesn't work on resolving the problems, but does everything he can to leave.'

Carlo and Luisa have two children, Davide, 8, and Katia, 14, both of whom find their father's fame a little tiring. What the father finds bothersome is that he doesn't get to see them enough. 'My fear is that my kids will get big without me even realizing it. That's the danger in this business.' And it's already happening, as his teenage daughter is almost as tall as he is. Although he works on Sunday, he's normally off on Monday, and does what he can to spend time with his kids.

'Since I don't see them a lot, I can't manage not to spoil them when I do,' he confessed. Ancelotti did manage to take them to see *Titanic* and *The Hunchback of Notre Dame*, and practically learned *The Lion King* by heart after seeing it four times on tape. But Carletto admitted that most of the cassettes he watches are of opposing teams, as he tries to prepare the following week's game. He normally pops in the tapes late at night, after he's put his kids to bed.

Luisa pushed Carlo to leave Sacchi and begin his own career as a coach. She doesn't regret it, either financially or personally, but worries about the toll it has taken on her husband. 'He's changed a lot since he's become a coach,' she says. 'As a player, all he had to worry about was himself. Now he has to take care of a dressing room filled with twenty-two players. That means a lot of pressure. He's also home about 50 per cent less than he was as a player.'

If Parma play at home on a Sunday, Carlo picks up his kids from the Catholic school they attend early Saturday afternoon, just like any other parent. They go home and the family has lunch together. Then Dad leaves for Saturday training. Since he spends the night with the team at a local hotel, the Toscanini, they won't be together again until after the game on Sunday. At the game, Katia sits with her friends in the *curva* with the rowdy fans; Luisa with the VIPs and players' wives; and Davide with his friends.

If Carlo hates to lose, Luisa hates it just as much for what it does to her husband. 'Ever since he's started coaching I've never really been at peace,' she confesses. 'Your life depends on results, and you live from Sunday to Sunday.' Even if Carlo appears calm in the post-game interviews after a loss, she knows that inside he's completely torn up. But there are a couple of minor victories on the home front that come with defeat. 'When they lose on Sunday, the most positive thing about it is that Carlo doesn't eat anything.' Luisa is always reminding him to watch his weight. 'He goes on a total diet. The other positive point is that he barricades himself inside the house with our kids. They talk, they play, but nobody's allowed to watch the sports programmes on TV.'

If Luisa is Ancelotti's biggest fan, she's also one of his harshest critics. 'I wish he were not such a nice guy,' she says. 'Rather than argue, he lets things go. If you look at the Roberto Baggio story, for example, he didn't say what he really thought right away.'

Milan wanted to get rid of Baggio, perhaps the most popular player in Italy. He was very close to coming to Parma at the beginning of the season, but Ancelotti blocked the deal. 'He should have told them he was really sceptical,' Luisa insisted. 'Instead it went all the way to the end, and he was forced to say "No!" straight out, but that got a lot of people angry with him.' Others agree with that critique of Carlo. 'A good coach has got to be a son-of-a-bitch sometimes,' said one reporter who has followed him closely. 'That's not Carlo's strong point.'

At the beginning of March, when the squad was long out of the Champions League, still in the Italian Cup, and tied for 5th place in the *campionato*, Parmalat chief Calisto Tanzi gave an interview to *La Gazzetta dello Sport* in which he said Ancelotti remained the coach, but that his future would depend on securing the team a place in Europe. The writing was on the wall, in four big black letters, UEFA.

Luisa was not impressed by the man who pays her husband nearly $1 million a year. 'If you meet these objectives, you remain; if not, you're out of here,' Luisa complained, as she summed up the evaluation of her husband. 'It's not very convincing. There are other owners who have unlimited confidence in their coaches. Look at Milan. Berlusconi says Capello's the coach and that's that. But Tanzi says Ancelotti . . . *if.*' (Ironically, Berlusconi's confidence wasn't without limits, and Capello was fired after a disappointing season.)

Ancelotti had a contract that was good through to June 2000, so if Tanzi sent him packing, he would still pick up a pretty hefty paycheque whether he was sitting at home, cultivating his vineyards, or planning his next management move. Luisa, who loves to travel, didn't hide her desire to go abroad. The kids, especially Katia, were against that prospect, though. They're happy in Parma and want to stay there.

'It's been a tough year for Carlo with the fans,' Luisa lamented at the beginning of March, during a rough spell for Parma. 'And it gets worse as it goes along. Jeering is now practically the order of the day. If it continues like this I'd suggest we get out of here. I figure that Carlo has about a fifty-fifty chance of remaining here.' Parma fans are notably tough. In other cities they adore you if you win and kill you if you lose. 'Here they jeer you no matter what you do,' Luisa said.

In the end it wasn't the fans who would seal Carlo's fate, but the owners. Little did he know it at the beginning of the season, when he had a fresh, three-year contract in hand, but by the last match, in May, Carlo would be out of a job.

Coaches change frequently in Italian football, and in Serie B nine out of twenty teams had replaced managers, some more than once, by early March. There are constant rumours about who's going where, and Ancelotti was not exempt from them. In both his first and second seasons at Parma, voices circulated that Ancelotti would be sacked.

In Ancelotti's first year at the Serie A squad, when the team quickly sank to the bottom of the standings, the wise men said owner Calisto Tanzi would bring back Nevio Scala, who had been let go after after seven seasons with the *gialloblu* (yellow and blues). Scala brought Parma into Serie A in 1990 and led them to four Cups over the next five years: the Italian Cup, the Cup Winners' Cup, the UEFA Cup, and the European Super Cup. Ancelotti survived the Scala scare, but only because his team started winning. They finished in 2nd place in the 1996–97 championship and were actually the strongest team in the 1997 calendar year.

Then in March of his second Parma season, while some commentators believed Ancelotti would get the boot, since Tanzi wanted to do better than 5th place, *La Gazzetta dello Sport* reported that he had been offered the Roma job. That would certainly have been a big temptation for Ancelotti. Although they have not won the *scudetto* since 1983, Roma are an important team in Serie A, with great fans and money to spend.

At the time, Ancelotti would only say that he had a contract with Parma for the next three years, and that he wanted to win something there before going anywhere else. He later denied that Roma had ever spoken with him, although the reporter from *Gazzetta* insisted his story was true. Asked again, Ancelotti repeated that he had never been contacted by Roma. He was, after all, happy at Parma.

And who wouldn't be? Parma, in northern Italy, with a population of 167,000, is a wealthy, pretty Italian city, not as big as nearby Bologna but not a village either. While the surrounding area is largely farmland, the city is best known for its ham, *prosciutto di Parma*, which is raw (cured for between nine and twelve months) and the best in Italy, if not in Europe. *Prosciutto di Parma* comes from the thigh of the pig, and is served in paper-thin slices. Its taste is slightly sweet. While it is the best known of the meats coming from the area, there is another prized one called 'culetto', literally 'botty'.

The city is also rich historically and artistically. Giuseppe Verdi was born in Parma, and the city's Royal Theatre is one of Italy's finest. Parma's public is terribly demanding, however, and some opera stars are afraid to perform there. As Ancelotti would learn, the city's football supporters were just as tough.

Football players don't generally spend a lot of nights out at the opera, or wander through the frescoed churches (Parma is home to some of Correggio's best work), but the city is a dream location for them all the same. They have the big-city comforts of Milan and Rome – great restaurants, good stores, lots of cinema – without any of the hassles. A traffic jam in Parma never lasts for more than ten minutes, and you can walk anywhere in the city centre in a matter of minutes. The players are left in peace. In most other Italian cities, and certainly the big ones, the local heroes don't go unnoticed. They get talked to, touched, and are constantly badgered for autographs, kisses and photographs. That Parma players are left in peace is good for them, but not great for the team overall. It's a sign that the supporters really aren't crazy about the squad. Fiorentina, Inter and even Bologna will get hundreds to show up for training sessions; Parma might get three or four or five people, in addition to a handful of journalists.

Bologna's Roberto Baggio is practically a recluse for this reason, and Fiorentina's manager Alberto Malesani reports that it's just not possible to stroll around Florence and do some casual shopping with his wife. 'They really make you feel like you're important here,' Malesani says, with a laugh. It was a major change for Malesani, who went to Fiorentina from Chievo, a tiny squad in Serie B. In Parma the players can get on with their lives, and go about their business without too many pressures. In what is really a sign of a small town, some of them walk home from the grounds. An occasional fan will ask for an autograph, but they don't get mobbed.

Parma's also a rich town, home not only to the team's sponsor, Parmalat, but also to Barilla. Together, they are two of the country's biggest food groups. Parmalat makes dairy products and biscuits and soups on six continents, whereas Barilla is the number-one Italian-owned food company, and the top pasta maker in the world. Years ago Barilla was sponsor for the Roma squad. Having a heavyweight owner/sponsor like Parmalat should be reassuring for a manager; they're not going to think twice about what they have to pay for a good player, and you don't have to go hunting for bargains or haggling excessively over contracts.

Parmalat weren't new to sports sponsorship when they put their name on the hometown team in 1988, then in Serie B. In 1985 they had sponsored Real Madrid, and since 1980 had been pouring millions of dollars into Formula One racing, sponsoring two champions, Nelson Piquet and Niki Lauda. Parma is one of Italy's baseball towns, along with Bologna, and the milk producers had also sponsored the local team, which has won the European championship.

Calisto Tanzi's office at Parmalat speaks almost as much as he does. It is small, impeccably clean, sparsely decorated and orderly to an extreme. The space could be transferred directly to a modern art museum or the showroom of a design company. Not a paper is out of place. Everything about the office – and about Tanzi himself – exudes a no-nonsense attitude. Tanzi, 58, speaks in short, clipped sentences. He had just returned from South Africa and was leaving the next day for the United States. Everything about his attire – grey suit, sky-blue shirt and dark tie – is perfect. Nothing loose, no collars sticking out, no scuffs on the black shoes. Calisto Tanzi is one serious corporate giant, much like Parmalat.

Tanzi, who founded and has built up the company into one of the world's largest producers of milk, yogurt and other dairy products, would have plenty of reason to be proud. He ranks among the wealthiest men in a wealthy country, and unlike many of the others on that list, his riches and success have come largely on account of his own efforts. But Tanzi tends to keep a low profile, giving few interviews and not blowing his own horn. Although he likes football, and goes to see Parma when he's not out of the country, he talks about the sport dispassionately, as if he were explaining the techniques to preserve or package milk, or expand his already vast Latin American market.

'The return on football is quite difficult to quantify; you don't know how much it's worth,' says Tanzi. He quickly adds, however, that the sport has undoubtedly given his company greater name recognition. 'Last year I was in Shanghai and looking at a Chinese magazine,' he notes. 'I couldn't understand a thing, but there was a photo of Zola with Parmalat written across his chest.'

The company has sponsored several teams in Latin America, including Palmeiras in Brazil, Universidad Católica in Chile and Boca Juniors in Argentina, all of which have won their respective league championships. 'The only one of our teams that hasn't won it is Parma,' he remarks, with dismay. But Italy's Serie A is at another level, and Tanzi acknowledges as much: 'I don't know if it's the most beautiful football championship in the world, but it's certainly among the most difficult.'

It's probably not the most beautiful, actually. Although Italian teams became a little more attack-minded a few years ago – when victory suddenly resulted in three points instead of only two – it's still a very defensive game. It was enough to see Inter this year; they had the best forward in the world, but won most of their games by tiny margins, and finished the season with fewer goals than Parma and Fiorentina, who took the last two UEFA places.

For a number of owners, a team in Serie A means that you've made it into a relatively closed Italian power structure. (You also need a seat in Parliament and either a newspaper or a television station. Berlusconi of Milan and Vittorio Cecchi Gori of Fiorentina are perfect examples.) Tanzi appears to have no interest in politics – although he is very good friends with a former Christian Democrat Prime Minister, Ciriaco De Mita. He's not the showman that Cecchi Gori and Berlusconi are, and his ego needs neither a newspaper or TV station. For Tanzi, football has been a very effective means of communication and marketing for his company, not himself.

A civic sense also moved Tanzi to purchase the squad, and he viewed his backing of Parma Calcio as a way of doing something for his hometown. But above all it is a way to spread his trademark, and sell more milk in twenty-five countries. Because Parmalat multinational holdings are so vast, European Cup competitions are more important to Tanzi than the Italian championship. 'But for the Italians, the city, the fans – and even our own personal satisfaction – it's a lot more important to win the *scudetto*,' he says.

Calisto Tanzi's 30-year-old son Stefano is president of the squad, and his daughter Francesca is also on the board of Parma Calcio. The football group is a business in itself and sponsors some 250 teams in Italy, where it can keep an eye on about 50,000 youngsters. Despite the financial power behind him (Parmalat-controlled companies have worldwide annual revenues of some £2.5 billion and employ 20,000 people) Stefano Tanzi might be too young to be running a football squad in Serie A. The directors at Juventus, for example, have been in the business longer than Stefano has been alive and professional football is full of sharks.

2 Ancelotti's Little Army

August, 1997. The season hadn't even begun and Ancelotti had a problem. It was called midfield. He had a superb keeper, an all-star defence, and a million-dollar attack, but something was missing in the middle. The guy who was going to push the ball up, get it to the goal scorers. What had gone wrong? It was a long story. There had been a number of phone calls the previous spring with Barcelona's Josep Guardiola, who kept saying, '*Sí, Sí, Sí.*' It was a done deal.

The Mister had asked Parma to buy Guardiola, and they did. Then Guardiola's '*sí*' became a 'no'. That was devastating for Ancelotti, who felt he had been screwed by Barca's midfielder. Ancelotti later reflected on the deal gone bad. He was upset about losing a talented player, but there was also a positive side to the story: 'If that's that way he acts, that's not the kind of guy I want playing for me.'

Someone had to fill the spot. Ancelotti had his hopes in Reynald Pedros, a 26-year-old Frenchman who had been highly touted when he was playing for Marseille. But little Pedros, who had been built up by Parma's directors as 'an important acquisition' showed no signs of stardom in the pre-season friendly matches. In fact, he didn't look very good at all. Add to that the problem that Pedros didn't speak Italian very well, and Ancelotti found himself with a melancholic Frenchman on his hands. Not a happy camper. And soon there were two melancholic Frenchmen. Another midfielder, Daniel Bravo, who spent seven years at Paris Saint-Germain, wasn't very happy either after he found himself sitting on the bench. By the end of October, there wasn't even room for him on the bench, and Bravo was watching Parma's games from the stands.

Pedros would be gone by Christmas, on loan to Napoli; Bravo went back to France, to Olympique Lyon. Pedros badmouthed Ancelotti at a press conference, claiming that the Mister didn't like foreigners. Bravo kept quiet but his wife, Eva, an Italian actress, took a shot at the Mister, claiming Ancelotti had not kept his promises for Daniel. Bravo at least got to play for a respectable team in France, whereas Pedros had terrible luck at Napoli, the worst squad in Serie A, and suffered more there than he had at Parma. Within a few months he too ended up at Olympique, who appeared to be on the lookout for disgruntled Frenchmen playing in Italy.

Hernán Crespo turned 22 at the beginning of the season. After a slow start the previous year he finally hit his stride, and finished with 11 goals. He celebrated with the purchase of a Ferrari Boxster, a fast, classy car with a $100,000 pricetag, a full step ahead of the BMWs that are practically part of the Parma uniform. The midnight blue Boxster was a symbol of Crespo's early success. But ten games into the '97–98 season, Crespo was already being booed by Parma fans, who thought he was missing goals he should have scored. He was still Parma's leading scorer with four goals, and Ancelotti defended the striker, stating publicly that if the fans ever boo a player, he'll be the last one to be yanked from the field. But even Ancelotti may have been having second thoughts about Crespo after he missed a couple of chances in the 0–2 loss to Roma at home at the end of November.

While Crespo was not having a great season, neither was his partner in attack, Enrico Chiesa. Parma, like most Italian teams, play with four defenders (two of whom are almost sweepers on the wings and used to bringing the ball upfield), four midfielders and two strikers. One of the strikers is normally a 'tower', someone tall and muscular, while the other is a fast, finesse player. Crespo is the tower; Chiesa the magician. That, at least, is the way it's supposed to work.

After ten games, there had not been a lot of magic; they had only 6 goals between them. Ronaldo had 8 goals for Inter at this point and Gabriel Batistuta of Fiorentina led the scoring with 10, a goal a game. Parma weren't scoring, but at least Ancelotti's stingy defence kept his squad competitive.

Chiesa was Parma's most expensive acquisition. They bought him from Sampdoria after the 1995–96 season for more than £6 million. He has provided some moments of excitement for the team, and at times played splendidly, with the same explosive energy that powered him to 22 goals in 27 games with Sampdoria. But Chiesa can be a whiner, and frequently complains that his team-mates don't give him the ball. In essence, a big $10 million baby.

To his credit, Chiesa did take responsibility for the Sparta goal that ruined Parma's chances for advancing in the Champions League, admitting that he should have been covering the scorer, Jiri Novotny. Even off the field, Chiesa tends to create problems. A football player has to go to one or two training sessions a day, and that's about the extent of his work, but on one occasion Chiesa was too 'busy' to visit the tailors to have his suit fitted; they had to come to the stadium for him.

Chiesa's role as a starter was not on the line when Parma suffered through their December crisis. If anybody was going to be sacrificed, it would be Crespo. And yet the blame could not all be laid on the Argentinian, and Ancelotti was unwilling to use him as the scapegoat. It was ironic that the fans would go after Crespo, who is cheerful, young and simpatico. He is also very handsome, or was, until he shaved his head at the beginning of the season. His buddy at Sampdoria, Juan Sebastian Veron, had done the same thing, and the Argentinians were apparently trying to start a new style. It didn't take off, and Crespo let his hair grow again.

Parma supporters showed exactly how fickle they were by jeering Crespo, who has a great attitude and could never be accused of slacking off, and backing Chiesa, the big complainer. When you miss a goal in Italy it's referred to as 'eating' it, and while Crespo had his share of chances gone bad, Chiesa ate more goals than anyone on Parma all season. Chiesa, convinced that he was always in the best position to score, also yelled at his companions whenever they failed to get him the ball. He's terribly quick and has a great foot on free-kicks, but the tiny attacker lacks the attitude of a team player.

Hernán Crespo has a personality that's nearly the opposite of Chiesa. He's outgoing, upbeat and positive. Rare were the moments this year when the Argentine complained about not getting a pass; he was more likely to applaud his team-mates, even if the shot went wide or they lost the ball. He'd clap a couple of times, nod and shake his fist, all to say, 'OK, good idea, we'll get it right next time.' The only occasion in which Crespo was less than generous came in February. He had gone seven games without a goal, and when Parma were awarded a penalty kick against Piacenza, Crespo insisted on taking it, even though on the list the Mister had drawn up, Chiesa was due to take the first one. But Crespo had been the one fouled, and he insisted on shooting. He scored, and, to his credit, Chiesa didn't make a fuss.

In midfield, two starters were always definite as long as they were healthy: Dino Baggio and Nestor Sensini in the central positions. On the wings, Ancelotti normally used Jesper Blomqvist and Massimo Crippa. Baggio, 26, is tall and strong and starts on the Italian national team. In the game that ensured Italy its berth in the World Cup, a 1–0 victory at Napoli, Baggio shadowed the Russian midfielder Dimitri Alenichev, shutting him down completely. Baggio looks like someone who doesn't really care about the game. He could be playing against Juventus – his former squad – or Milan, and he'll have this look on his face that says, 'OK, let's get it over with.' But Ancelotti says that look is deceiving, and that Baggio concentrates and plays with great intensity: 'Dino's the kind of guy you need to give real precise instructions to. Let him know what his role is and don't give him too many things to do, and he'll work just fine.' He's often referred to as 'Big Baggio' to distinguish him from the little guy with the same surname, Roberto Baggio. Dino Baggio has a good head on corner kicks and a powerful shot, but his real value lies more on defence than attack. After ten games of the regular season he had scored just one goal.

Baggio can kid his boss goodnaturedly, and when Ancelotti missed a pre-season training session,* the midfielder remarked, 'Thank God he's not around to bust our balls today.' Ancelotti's response: 'He should talk.' But deep down Baggio has great esteem for Ancelotti, and vice versa. He would follow his Mister just about anywhere in Serie A, and Ancelotti would probably take him.

Nestor Sensini is another solid piece of midfield machinery who has seen his share of battles. The 31-year-old Argentinian came to Parma in 1993 after five seasons with Udinese. Sensini is one of four players in the squad Ancelotti labels a *trascinatore*, a natural leader. The Argentinian has also picked up Italian citizenship, which makes it easier for him to play in Italy, since a squad can only have three non-EC residents on the pitch and on the bench. Sensini's absence on account of injury may have played a role in Parma's loss to Roma and dismal draw with Sparta. Ancelotti certainly thought so.

Not surprisingly for a team known for not giving up a lot of goals, the other three 'leaders' normally find themselves on Parma's side of the pitch during a game: keeper Gianluigi Buffon and defenders Lilian Thuram and Fabio Cannavaro. 'Fabio,' said the Mister, 'is someone I would let marry my daughter.' And given Cannavaro's good looks and pleasant personality, Katia Ancelotti would probably be all for such an arrangement, but Cannavaro is already married.

On the midfield wings, Pietro Strada's injury put him out for the season, and Parma were forced to go shopping. They picked up Jesper Blomqvist, a Swede, from Milan. Blomqvist played well,

---

* A typical training session – they are normally in the afternoon – takes an hour and a half and consists of jogging, various ball-control drills, one-on-one challenges in front of the goal, tactical plans and small scrimmages. It ends with 10 minutes of stretching. On Wednesday there are two sessions; the one in the morning is for working out with weights.

at times exceptionally in his first few games, but it was clear he wouldn't be the kind of guy to turn the season around for Parma. Blomqvist, small and quick, has good feet and played in 27 games but scored just 1 goal. Low key and even-keeled, Blomqvist likes to golf on his day off. On the other wing Ancelotti frequently used Massimo Crippa, a chunky, physical player who never scores a lot of goals (he had one each season in '95–96 and '96–97) but can create problems for the opposing midfield.

Crippa has been in the first division since 1987 and knows all the strengths and weaknesses of the other teams. His own strength is an asset in intimidating other squads, and he's built like a freight train. Crippa's muscle often makes him more of a troublemaker than an opportunity maker for Parma, and he carries the rather dubious distinction as the most hated of all Parma players in Serie A. None of them are booed as much as Crippa. He's definitely not simpatico, but he's solid. And Ancelotti admires his attitude. 'I'd take a team of eleven Crippas any day of the week,' the Mister said. 'Massimo always gives everything he's got, and you can't say that about a lot of players.'

Ancelotti was anxiously awaiting the return of Federico Giunti, who missed the first nine games of the season on account of injury. The Mister was hoping Giunti would provide that extra spark on the offensive side of midfield and frequently referred to Giunti as 'our Guardiola'. Giunti played satisfactorily in his first few games, but it was clear that it would take several seasons for young Giunti to become a Guardiola, if it was to happen at all.

In defence, Ancelotti relied above all on the finesse and maturity of Lilian Thuram, a tall, softspoken stopper who was born on the island of Guadeloupe. Thuram came to Parma in 1996 after six seasons with Monaco, and was one of six players in Serie A this season who were starting on the French national team. Although Sensini is the captain of Parma, Thuram – considered by many to be the best defender in the game today – commands tremendous authority and is a favourite among the fans.

Thuram, who as a boy considered studying for the priesthood, likes the respect he's granted as an experienced full-back known for playing clean. He earns that respect, and usually has the task of marking the other team's star striker. In the duel with Inter's Ronaldo he held his own, and could hardly be faulted for Ronaldo's goal, which decided the game. Thuram wears glasses off the field, which gives him something of an intellectual look, but he's just one of the boys, and stands out more for his skill than his demeanour. 'See you poofters later,' he'll tell his buddies on leaving training.

Alongside Thuram plays Fabio Cannavaro, Parma's poster-boy. A handsome blond Neapolitan, Cannavaro has the face of a *scugnizzo*, or Naples street urchin, both shrewd and simpatico at the same time. Cannavaro's stock rose considerably when he shut down Alan Shearer in the Italian national team's 1−0 victory over England at Wembley. As full-backs, or wing-backs, Ancelotti normally uses a Brazilian, Zé Maria, and Antonio Benarrivo. Zé Maria, 24, came to Parma in 1996, whereas the 29-year-old Benarrivo has spent all of his first division years with the squad and is coming to the end of his career.

In goal stands the baby of the team. Gianluigi Buffon turned 20 in January 1998. But before celebrating that he had already earned himself a place on the Italian national team. He came in out of the cold in Moscow to replace the injured Gianluca Pagliuca, and immediately made a diving stop in the muck to save the game for the Italians and get them into the World Cup. Ancelotti believes he has two of the best players in the world in Thuram and Buffon. Thuram has already been tried and tested, and Buffon certainly looks like he's on the road to glory. If it doesn't come with Parma then it might come with Italy.

If Buffon is one of Parma's bright lights, one of the dark spots is the back-up to the back-up keeper, Luca Bucci. A local favourite, Bucci was born in nearby Bologna and played with Parma in the late 1980s when they were still in the second division. He came back when Parma were promoted in 1993 and was the first-choice keeper for three straight seasons. But Ancelotti made a tough decision in his first year with the squad, that the 18-year-old Buffon − barely old enough for a driver's licence in Italy − would be starting in goal. Bucci's contract was good through June of 1998, and it was tough for someone who had gone to the World Cup in Los Angeles to think that he would be sitting on the bench for the next couple of years while the new wonderkid manned the nets.

It wasn't an easy decision for Ancelotti, but the Mister had no doubts that Buffon had proven himself a better goalkeeper, and he told Bucci as much. Bucci reacted badly, and asked for a transfer. He was loaned to Perugia for the season and came back in July 1997. Several months away helped heal the wounds, and the goalkeeper apologized to Ancelotti for his earlier comments, but he still wasn't happy back at Parma. Like a number of older players whose glory days are behind them, Bucci was simply going through the motions – training, meetings, retreats – and not trying too hard to put on a happy face.

Torino finally ended the agony in mid-season. There Bucci got to play, and did well, helping the squad make its run for promotion to Serie A. In his later years at Parma Bucci had given the impression he was a piece of dead wood being carried along by the current. At 29 he was one of the older players, not on the same wavelength as the rest of the team. They don't play or they play very little, and they have nothing to look forward to.

Bucci is small with curly hair and a beard, quiet and cat-like, while Buffon is a towering kid with an easy smile, built like an American football player or a basketball forward. Bucci was still good, but it was simply clear that Buffon was even better. And although Bucci was popular, Buffon rapidly won the hearts of the fans, and gets more mail each week than any other player on the squad. (Buffon gets about 10 letters a day. Then comes Dino Baggio, who's well known internationally, and Fabio Cannavaro.)

Another player in the twilight of his career was defender Luigi Apolloni, who has been with Parma since 1987, again when the team were still in the second division. Apolloni also played on the World Cup side that finished second in Los Angeles, and although he has never won the *scudetto* he was in the Parma squad that

captured the UEFA Cup in 1995. Not a hot-rod, Apolloni sometimes rides to practice on a scooter while all the others showed
up in their Mercedes and BMWs.

Alessandro Melli, 28, a tall, powerful striker, built more like a
basketball player than a footballer, was in a similar position. He
saw very little playing time in '97–98, before being acquired by
Serie B side Perugia. Bucci, Apolloni and Melli all had contracts
with Parma that expired at the end of June 1998, but Apolloni
was the only one who played his out.

If the players getting ready to hang up their boots sometimes
showed their dismay, that was offset by the enthusiasm and energy
of the youngsters, especially two strikers, Filippo Maniero and
Bolzan Adailton. Maniero, 25, was the 'tower'; Adailton, 20, the
quick little thing. Both got to play in the early part of the season,
when Parma were also competing in the Champions League and
the Italian Cup, and both managed to score goals.

Although they could have complained privately that they were
not seeing enough time on the pitch, Maniero and Adailton didn't
do so publicly. They worked hard, and made every effort to make
the Mister believe that they'd be ready when he was ready for
them. Adailton was just a kid, and usually had a sheepish smile on
his face. He only got into trouble once, and that was a minor
scrape with the law. Police in Parma pulled him over on his scooter
and found out he didn't have any insurance. The engaging smile
almost worked as Adailton explained to the cops that in Brazil
nobody carries insurance for scooters.

Adailton and Maniero were rewarded for having the right attitude, but in different ways. By the end of January, Maniero had
been sold to Milan, who were was weak in attack after George
Weah's injury and Patrick Kluivert's painfully slow start. Maniero
scored a goal in his first game dressed in red and black, and Adailton
started to see some playing time as Ancelotti tried to fix Parma's
scoring crisis.

Parma's supposed big fix came on January 15, when they com-
pleted negotiations with Newcastle for Faustino Asprilla, the Colombian striker. With only 26 points they were a full 10 points

behind league leaders Inter, and club owner Calisto Tanzi wanted results. Asprilla was a risky choice, however. He had been sold by Parma two years earlier after a series of off-the-field incidents.

In his first stay at Parma,★ Asprilla had a fling with a local showgirl in Parma, Petra Sharbach, which triggered the separation from his wife. And he picked up the nickname 'Tino el Pistolero' after celebrating New Year's by firing a gun in the air. He also returned from Colombia once with several stitches in his leg. The official line on the cut was that he had fallen on glass near a pool, but no one believed that. Even before he went off to Newcastle, Asprilla's stock had dropped considerably. 'Tino el Pistolero' was also hampered by injuries while in England, and Parma had no guarantee that he had recovered. But Tanzi paid more than $10 million to get him back, and he apparently believed that Asprilla could work miracles for his squad.

Asprilla's return got mixed reviews. Everyone on the team, starting with the coach, said it was good news. That was the official line. Striker Hernán Crespo liked the idea that somebody would now be getting the ball to him. Ancelotti put on a happy face, but it was unclear whether he was as excited about the newcomer as Calisto Tanzi was. And this time he wouldn't have had the power to block the move, as he did with Baggio over the summer. The owner's 30-year-old son, Stefano Tanzi, president of the team, had said, just a couple of weeks earlier, 'We don't like reheated soup.' But you learn to like it if that's what your pop is paying for. 'Parma is prisoner of its happy past,' said the Rome daily *La Repubblica*. 'In times of disorientation it's the reactionary instinct that takes control.'

If Asprilla didn't score goals, at least he would bring excitement. But the hope was that 'Tino' could do both. Fans remembered that it was he who broke Milan's 53-game unbeaten streak in March of 1993 with a dazzling free-kick. And they remembered

★ On arriving in Parma in 1992, Asprilla was so impressed by the shiny chrome in a home appliances store that he bought two boxes of bathroom fixtures to send back to relatives in Colombia.

the cartwheels he'd do to celebrate each of his goals. Faustino Asprilla would bring personality and offensive punch to Ancelotti's solid, serious, defensive squad. That was the hope, anyway. In Serie A first time around, Asprilla had scored 25 goals in 84 games. At Newcastle he had 24 goals over two years, but was plagued by injuries. So the move was not without its risks.

Where to put the Colombian? Ancelotti's team managed to stay among the top four by giving up very few goals. Inserting Asprilla in the front line would mean changing to a 3–4–3 formation, with a three-man attack, or staying with a 4–4–2 but inserting Asprilla in midfield in the place of Jesper Blomqvist. And that may have been more likely. Ancelotti, stubborn as he is, wouldn't readily change from a 4–4–2 to a 3–4–3 in mid-season.

Tanzi had gambled $10 million on the Colombian. And Parma fans were right to ask questions: why do you go after Asprilla after you've let Zola go and refused Roberto Baggio? Parma sold Zola to Chelsea because the price was right and they had bought Enrico Chiesa, who they expected to become their scoring machine. Milan wanted to unload the ageing Baggio during the summer, but Ancelotti nixed the deal. Why? Baggio needed to make a good show during the season before the 1998 World Cup and would not have been happy sitting on the bench. Ancelotti didn't have an immediate starting position for 'Roby' and didn't want problems.

When the Asprilla deal was announced, Ancelotti made it clear that he considered the Colombian a more flexible player than either Baggio or Zola. 'And above all he's content to be part of a group that includes Chiesa and Crespo,' the Mister said. 'That would not have been the case with either Baggio or Zola.' Unfortunately, Asprilla, who was bothered by a groin injury, would see very little playing time and made more noise off then field than on it. Racing to training one afternoon in his BMW he hit a woman in a tiny Fiat. She ended up in hospital, and Parma's spokesman and all around fix-it man, Giorgio Bottaro, spent the afternoon with her. Fortunately, she had only minor injuries, but the Fiat was destroyed. Not exactly a reason for a cartwheel.

3 Something's Got to be Fixed

Most of Ancelotti's players address him with the familiar 'tu' in Italian and not the formal 'lei', which is more distant and respectful. On some other squads, such as Marcello Lippi's Juventus, the players use the form of respect. Ancelotti has not yet turned 40 and is closer in age to his players than Lippi, and it's also a matter of style. Ancelotti takes part in some of the training scrimmages and drills, and doesn't simply direct them. And yet, he's not the player-coach, and there's a clear distinction between him and his boys. Even if they use the familiar second-person 'you' they still tend to call him 'Mister' rather than Carlo, as a sign of respect.

Even at their usual training field, La Certosa, an old monastery that's been converted into a school for prison guards, the coaches have a separate dressing room. There's a certain distance between players and coach, but it's relatively minor at Parma, and the boys can horse around with Ancelotti at training, but they know not to push it.

When Parma played in Bari in an Italian Cup match in the autumn, someone gave a big crate of fresh mozzarella cheese to Ancelotti, who's known for appreciating good food. On the flight back that night, several players were hungry and dipped into Ancelotti's goods, substituting the cheese they ate with newspapers. The Mister only discovered the theft after he was back home, but took it well. 'Thank God I didn't give it to anyone as a gift,' he said.

While the Mister was curious to find out who'd munched his mozzarella (he never did) he didn't make a federal case over it, or launch an official investigation. The fact that it could happen at Parma indicated the kind of relationship there was beween players and coach. No one would have ever dreamed of doing such a thing with Arrigo Sacchi, Marcello Lippi or Fabio Capello. The culprits were at the limit with Ancelotti, and wouldn't want to push it any further than a box of cheese, but that was good-natured and good fun, and the kind of thing that can take some of the pressure off a very intense season. But that was the catch, the pressure, the constant need to prove to the owners and the fans that you could win the *scudetto*. If a manager didn't have that need to succeed, running a squad in Serie A could actually be fun.

The first real test for Ancelotti and Parma came in the seventh game of the regular season at San Siro Stadium in Milan. Inter, bolstered by nearly a goal a game from the Brazilian standout Ronaldo, were in 1st place with 16 points; Parma had four wins and two draws, leaving them with 14 points and level in 2nd place with Juventus. A victory against Inter would push Parma into 1st place, and a draw would at least keep Inter from running away.

But San Siro isn't an easy place for visiting teams. A huge stadium with a field full of divots, it was filled to near capacity for Parma's visit, and 70,000 hostile fans were in place to jeer the visitors. The crowd had plenty of practice getting rowdy before the game started, and whistled energetically every time Milan defender Paolo Maldini's face flashed on to the electronic screen for an Opel advertisement. Some Italian women may be so swayed by Maldini's good looks that they'll buy Opel station wagons, but they won't be Inter fans.

Internazionale had not won the *campionato* since Lothar Matthäus brought them to the top in 1989, and were desperate for it from the very start of the season. Against Parma they controlled the pace of the game from the first minute. The fans roared every time Ronaldo even got near the ball. And within the first 15 minutes of the game the young man known as 'the Phenomenon' showed why he's worth whatever it is that Inter and Nike and Pirelli pay him. When he doesn't have the ball he looks like he's lazy, just standing around. But apparently he's saving all his energy for when his foot touches leather. Once it does, he accelerates like

44

no other striker in the game today. When Ronaldo takes off, especially as he likes to, diagonally, no one defender is going to stop him without fouling him.

Parma just couldn't take control. Their defence held up, but the team was getting overrun in midfield, which the Brazilian Zé Elias controlled. Parma were suffering their first case of the nerves, playing chase, and forced to foul. Dino Baggio tripped up Zé Elias just outside the penalty area 15 minutes into the first half and Inter had a free-kick. Or more precisely, Ronaldo had a free-kick. He shot with his instep, lifting the ball over four leaping Parma players who made up the wall, and curled it into the upper right-hand corner. Gianluigi Buffon, stranded near the far post, never moved. 1–0, Inter, and Ronaldo had just scored his sixth goal in seven league games.

Ancelotti would argue later that it was a bad call that set up the goal, and complained about the two yellow cards that Parma picked up in the first half. He may have gotten some bad decisions, but it really didn't matter, Parma were behind 1–0 in enemy territory, and Inter were playing one of their best games of the season. And that's how it would end, although Inter had a few other chances to widen their lead. Buffon made a stunning save from a breakaway by Taribo West, and Thuram was nearly flawless in defence, despite the double threat of Ronaldo and Youri Djorkaeff. Ancelotti blamed the goal – but not the game – on the official.

Several Parma matches were decided in midfield. When it worked, the squad worked, and when it didn't everything else fell apart. Ancelotti's team boasted a good attack and a great defence, but if the four midfielders couldn't get the ball to strikers and protect the backs, all was lost. Ancelotti builds his squad upon the premise that it has to be physical and aggressive, and if that's missing in midfield, it shows.

This became particularly evident against Sampdoria and Brescia in the first half of the season. Against Sampdoria, Juan Sebastian Veron and Alain Boghossian seemed to operate without disturbance, continually serving the ball up to their strikers, especially Vincenzo Montella. Ironically, Parma got a great game out of their star defenders, Cannavaro and Thuram, but it didn't seem to matter, as Samp managed to score five goals anyway.

Something similar happened with Brescia. The midfield showed its muscle, but was unable to create any attacking opportunities. Blomqvist might as well have not been in the match. Ancelotti couldn't understand it. The week before, his entire team came roaring after Milan; seven days later they lost to a modest club, and even the pillars of the defence, Cannavaro and Thuram, looked like they were out of shape. Cannavaro was forced to foul Dario Hubner in the area and Brescia sneaked away with a victory. But the entire match couldn't be blamed on the midfield and defence; Crespo twice missed opportunities that would have given the *gialloblu* the lead.

When the midfield worked, Parma won, or at least drew. This was true against Juventus in November, when Blomqvist played a great game, continually getting by Alessandro Birindelli to bring the ball up and cross. Dino Baggio, Nestor Sensini and Federico Giunti were also hungry for a victory, continually pressing forward and successfully thwarting Zinedine Zidane. Parma drew 2–2 but could have easily won had Chiesa closed it for them. In defence, Cannavaro kept Inzaghi under control and Thuram covered Del Piero like a rug.

Blomqvist proved fundamental in Parma's 3–1 victory over Milan in January as well. Even though the goals came from Chiesa and Dino Baggio, the Swede was continually creating scoring occasions. Stefano Fiore also played a solid 90 minutes in midfield as Ancelotti's boys shut down the likes of Ibrahim Ba, Leonardo and Dejan Savicevic.

If Parma had been nervous and confused in their 1–0 loss to Inter, the best way to bounce back would come with a convincing victory at Dortmund in the Champions League four days later. Dortmund had won the championship the previous year when they upset Juventus, but they had not been as convincing this season. Parma beat them in the first leg at home 1–0, and went into this game fairly confident. Dortmund, despite the presence

of veterans Andy Möeller and Paulo Sousa in midfield, and Julio
Cesar in defence, found themselves floundering in the Bundesliga.
Möeller, Sousa and Julio Cesar are all former Juventus players; and
Dortmund's coach is an Italian, Nevio Scala. It was Scala, of course,
who brought Parma from Serie B to Serie A, and put the squad
on the international football map.

Parma played well for the first 30 minutes and then began to
collapse. Midfielder Pietro Strada went out with a knee injury,
and the squad seemed to lose all offensive drive. Möeller and Sousa
controlled the pace of the game, and it was only a matter of time
before Borussia put the ball in the net. Parma's defence played
below their normal level, and Cannavaro was forced to foul in
the penalty area at the 35th minute. But Buffon made a brilliant
save from Stephane Chapuisat, and Parma were still in the game.
And they managed to stay in the game when a linesman mistakenly
signalled offside for a Chapuisat goal. The first half finished 0–0.

Borussia got on the scoreboard only five minutes into the second
half from a Möeller free-kick. Parma had disappeared. Nothing
worked up front, and there was no inspiration from midfield. At
the 30-minute mark, Cannavaro again fouled in the area and
Möeller lined up to take the penalty. Buffon guessed the direction
and stopped the shot, but Möeller made good on the rebound.
And so it finished 2–0. Ancelotti just had his worst week since
the Champions League competition began nearly three months
earlier. Parma dropped to 2nd in Group A of the Champions
League, two points behind Borussia. They now needed victories
against Sparta Praga, played at home, and at Galatasaray, if they
were going to stay in it. Juventus were also in 2nd place, in Group
B, three points behind Manchester United.

Strada's knee injury against Borusssia would keep him sidelined
for nearly the entire season, and Parma's problems in midfield
went from serious to grave. And that was only one of Ancelotti's
difficulties. 'We've got problems all over, from the keeper to the
strikers,' he said. 'We're not playing like a team. Here at Dortmund
we played well for a half-hour, and that was it. After Buffon
stopped Chapuisat's penalty shot, I saw only one team on the field,

and that was Dortmund. Möeller and Sousa created difficulties for us, and we took a dive both physically and psychologically.'

Ancelotti talked about the hustle and organization that had made Parma so competitive in the second half of the previous season as if they had been temporarily misplaced. 'Parma's a team that has to keep its concentration at the maximum,' the Mister noted. 'Unfortunately, I see a lot of superficiality.' If only everyone could play with that Sacchi-like intensity, always looking like they were about to witness an apparition of the Virgin Mary.

Italian newspapers give grades to players after every game, and most of Parma flunked the Dortmund test. The numbers range from 5 to 10, and the Rome daily *La Repubblica* gave plenty of 5s and 6s. Only keeper Gianluigi Buffon managed to earn an 8. *La Gazzetta dello Sport* was slightly more generous, but not much. An 8 for Buffon, 7 for Strada, while the much feared defence picked up 5.5s and 6s. Only Buffon played a great game, and he still gave up two goals.

'Somebody who stops two penalty shots at Dortmund can do absolutely anything,' *La Gazzetta* gushed. 'The next Michael Jordan, or something between Superman and Batman. He's only got to choose. Parma hopes he continues to be a footballer.' But *La Gazzetta*'s opinion of Ancelotti's squad as a whole lacked that enthusiasm. 'The joy of the start of the season seems to have disappeared in the cold and dark of Dortmund,' it said. 'The wounds are there, and it's not going to be easy to heal them. If Parma were once used to scoring at will, now they can't even find the goal. Something's got to be fixed.' And yet, Parma, stingy Parma, had never really been used to scoring at will, and that was one of the Mister's worries. True, they had beaten Udinese 4–0 in September, but that was the exception, not the rule, and Ancelotti joked after that match that he didn't know what had happened to Parma.

If Ancelotti wanted consolation, he needed only to look at the previous season. Seven games into it Parma found themselves fifth from the bottom. That was Ancelotti's first season in Serie A, and no one would have been surprised had he been sacked. But Parma stuck with him, and that proved to be the right move. The rookie coach stubbornly led the team nearly to the top of the standings. They beat Milan at San Siro just before Christmas and would finish the season in 2nd place, 5 points in front of Roy Hodgson's Inter and just a single point behind a brilliant Juventus.

The following Sunday Parma won at home, 2−0 against Empoli. That was just a kind of warm-up match for the following week's game at Juventus.

Juventus may or may not have been the strongest team in the world, as Ancelotti believed a little more than two months into the season. But the black and whites nearly lost to Parma, and three days later got blown off the field in Rotterdam when Feyenoord blanked them 2−0 in the Champions League. Ancelotti still bet on them to win the Italian League Championship, predicting the season to finish 1) Juventus 2) Parma 3) Milan 4) Inter.

How were Inter − so far unbeaten − going to go from 1st to 4th place? 'Inter are playing over their heads,' the Mister said. 'Ronaldo has brought them all up a notch, but that can't last.' Those words sounded almost prophetic when just days later Strasbourg dominated Ronaldo and Inter, beating the *nerazzuri* (black and blues) 2−0 in the UEFA Cup. And yet Inter would later come back to beat Strasbourg.

Parma had Cup problems of their own. They were hit by injuries for the November 27 match against Sparta Praga. Several first-choice players, including almost the entire midfield, were absent. Jesper Blomqvist hadn't been with Parma long enough for eligibility for the Champions League; he could start playing in March if Parma were still in it. Massimo Crippa, Parma's intimidator, had two yellow cards in previous games, and Pietro Strada was out for the season with torn ligaments. Nestor Sensini would miss the game because of a strained muscle, and would probably have to sit out the regular season match against Roma as well. In defence, Fabio Cannavaro twisted an ankle in training and was expected to miss the game, and Antonio Benarrivo was also out with an injury.

Veteran Luigi Apolloni would substitute for Cannavaro and

Mauro Milanese for Benarrivo to fill in the back four. Milanese, 26, with his unkempt hair, has a scraggily look to him, and plays somewhat scraggily as well. He can hold his own as full-back, but won't be a regular start in a major Serie A squad. At midfield Federico Giunti would join Dino Baggio at the central positions while Mario Stanic and Stefano Fiore would take up the wings. Stanic had been outstanding the previous season until he was injured in a friendly while playing for Croatia.

His comeback this season would be mixed. His wife and baby son were in Croatia and that seemed to weigh on 'Big Mario'. He didn't have his head in the game, which showed in the kind of passes made, and he got booed early on by Parma supporters. When the Mister later moved him up to forward, Stanic's play improved, and he scored 3 goals in 5 games in February and March. Meanwhile, Fiore, 22, had played in Serie B the previous season, at Chievo, and was getting his first real chance to show his stuff at Parma.

If something needed to be fixed, or at least retouched, on Parma, it was still the midfield. While Dino Baggio plays a good, solid game, especially shutting down the oppostion's playmaker, Parma didn't have a *regista* or director, a kind of commander who has vision of the entire field and knows how to push the ball up by making the right pass, short or long, or bringing it up himself.

Milan midfielder Demetrio Albertini and the Frenchman Didier Deschamps of Juve both play this role brilliantly, or at least they once did. But neither was on the market when Ancelotti was looking. Parma were also missing the *fantasista*, also called a *mezza-punta*, someone who can play in between midfield and the attack, setting up the ball for the strikers. Zinedine Zidane of Juventus can fill that *fantasista* role perfectly. Gianfranco Zola used to play in this position at Parma, but wanted to score goals and make money and went off to Chelsea.

And then, of course, there had been the chance to sign Roberto Baggio, the best-known and best-loved of all Italian playmakers . . .

'Attack!' was Ancelotti's order against Sparta Prague, and the team responded in what was to be Parma's best and worst game so far this year. Everything worked smoothly early on as Parma pressed, pressed and then some more. Despite all of the missing starters, the team looked better than it had all season. Enrico Chiesa's early goal on a perfect pass from Federico Giunti put Parma in the lead. It was an excellent start.

But, in what would become a seemingly chronic problem, they couldn't connect for the second goal. The Czech goalkeeper, Tomas Postulka, made several excellent saves, and Parma wasted other chances. Crespo headed one high, and Stanic scored, but the goal was disallowed for offside. Postulka stymied shots by Fiore, Stanic and Baggio. Thuram, a central defender and perhaps the best player on the pitch, brought the ball upfield on several occasions, and Parma continued to play aggressively for nearly the entire game, but they couldn't manage to close it. Then came the 90th minute.

Had the whistle blown, Parma would have walked off the field with a victory and some chance of qualifying for the quarter-finals of the Champions League. Instead, another three goals were scored over the next 6 minutes in a bizarre finish. Sparta put the ball in the net on 91 minutes from a header by Jiri Novotny, and Parma saw their future disappear. As if to rub it in, on a counter-attack 2 minutes later, Sparta scored again when an unmarked Josef Obajdin put the ball in the net. In the sixth minute of injury time, Parma were awarded a penalty and Enrico Chiesa got his second goal of the game to salvage a 2–2 draw.

But a draw was as good as a loss when Parma had to win at all costs. The final whistle blew and the fans jeered their team. Ancelotti was dejected after a victory that his boys let slip away. 'We played a great game, and were at the top of our form,' he said. 'We paid the price for the two times when we weren't careful in defence. And we failed to nail down a victory that should have been nailed down.'

During this season Ancelotti would see clearer than ever before that football isn't always fair. Parma had 12 shots on goal and scored 2; Sparta put in 2 out of 4. A great game, but only up to a point. The strikers and midfielders couldn't keep blowing their chances, and the entire team had not yet learned how to keep a lead. Something still had to be fixed.

Three days' rest were not enough to fix Parma's problems, and they were right back in the thick of it the following Sunday, playing at home against Roma. Ancelotti knew the team would be tired, but at least thought they'd be angry after the disappointing outing with Sparta. For a football fan, it was a great game: lots of action, good saves, what the Italians call plenty of *spettacolo*. It was a spectacle, all right. At one point Buffon stopped four shots, none of them easy, in the course of 20 seconds. It was end-to-end stuff: Parma had 11 shots on goal; Roma had 10. And once again it was the other team that had the killer instinct. Roma scored at the 9th and the 22nd minute, and that's all it took for a 2−0 victory away from home. Roma, playing with three strikers, like fast football with plenty of goalmouth action. Parma had their chances on the counter-attack but failed to capitalize.

Against Sparta, Ancelotti saw his chances to advance in the Champions League melt away; after Sunday's game he began seeing his chance for the *scudetto* starting to slide. Roma's victory gave them three points and put them in 3rd place. After ten games the top of the table looked like this:

INTER	26
JUVENTUS	22
ROMA	19
UDINESE	19
PARMA	18

Fiorentina's Gabriel Batistuta was top scorer with 10 goals − one a game − followed by Baggio, Ronaldo and Abel Balbo of Roma, each with 8. Parma's top scorer was Hernán Crespo with 4. While the fans were angry with Crespo, Ancelotti stood by the Argentinian, even though he admitted that the striker was not at the top of his form. The previous season, it took a while for

52

Crespo to get 'unblocked'. Once he did, he was a powerhouse, and finished the season with 11 goals.

Parma's Mister could have substituted Crespo with either of his youngsters on the bench, Filippo Maniero or the Brazilian Bolzan Adailton. Both had the right attitude, a great desire to prove themselves. In the end he decided to stick with Crespo, sure that he would eventually find his form. But Ancelotti was beginning to worry. Were Parma destined to suffer bad starts every season?

The manager also needed to fill in holes in defence. He didn't like the way Brazilian Zé Maria was playing and had used 34-year-old veteran Roberto Mussi several times in his place. Zé Maria – who happened to be a buddy and a kind of big brother to Ancelotti's young son Davide – took it badly. The Brazilian's agent told Ancelotti that the player wasn't happy at Parma, and wanted to change teams. Ancelotti and Zé Maria had a long talk in which the Mister said, 'I'm not playing you because you're not in top form. I promise you that if you put out in practice you'll be a starter again.' Zé Maria had to admit that he wasn't giving 100 per cent, but promised to apply himself. He apparently did, and shortly afterwards was in the starting line-up once again. And his agent stopped talking about a transfer.

4 The (New) Competition: Lazio, Udinese, Fiorentina

The classic Italian derby takes place between Juventus and Inter, the only two teams that have never been relegated to Serie B. Between them, they've garnered 37 championships in 100 years of Italian football. Milan recently passed up Inter in the number of *scudetti* (15 to 13) but are still a new kid on the block compared to the other two. Between the 1989–90 season and 1996–97, Milan won the *scudetto* four times and finished 2nd twice. In the same period, Juventus won twice and finished 2nd three times. Inter had not won for ten years, but Massimo Moratti was betting all his marbles on his new, Ronaldo-led squad.

On paper, the *scudetto* looked like it would be a three-way race. But it didn't work out that way, at least not in the beginning, largely because Milan drew or lost most of their opening games and dropped out of sight. After they lost to Lecce in October, they were in 13th place. That afternoon Capello was furious, with the team, the referee, apparently with the world. He left the pitch shouting at the ref like a madman.

Ancelotti refused to write off the *rossoneri*, or red and blacks, so soon. His reasoning came partly from a sentimental attachment to Milan, partly from experience. 'We were even further out of it at this point last season, and came back to finish 2nd,' he said. 'Let's wait and see.' And, initially, he was right; by the mid-point of the season, Milan had clawed their way back into the top half of the table.

If Milan were a disappointment, so were Parma. In the last four games of the first leg of the championship, they had tied one, lost two, and managed to win only one, a 3−1 victory over Milan. In the first five matches of the return, they had just two victories and three draws. In nine games they had amassed only 13 points, and the newspapers were already beginning to talk about Ancelotti getting yanked.

Surprisingly, the *gialloblu* weren't out of it completely, and the Mister still held out hope for a 2nd-place finish and a berth in the Champions League. After 22 games, and with 12 to go, Parma were level in 5th place with Fiorentina and Roma, and had 38 points. Juventus, which had taken the lead from Inter at mid-season as Ronaldo slumped, was in 1st place with 48 points.

Inter followed with 44 points, but were tied for 2nd place with Lazio. And Udinese, with their three-pronged attack led by Oliver Bierhoff, were nipping at their heels, with 42 points. Lazio? Udinese? These were the two surprises of 1997−98, and both were in the running for the *scudetto*. Ironically, they were both teams that Parma had held its own against in the first half of the season. Ancelotti's boys beat Udinese 4−0 in September when their defence shut down Bierhoff, and they had drawn with Lazio 1−1 in January. But that was one of Lazio's few draws in recent months, and they had not lost since December 7, against Juventus. In the next 15 games − both league and Cup competition − Lazio won an extraordinary 13 and drew 2.

Lazio, coached by Sven Goran Eriksson, have frequently pretended to reach great heights, but rarely managed to do so. In nearly seventy years of existence, the 'Eagles' have won the *scudetto* only once, in 1973−74, under the leadership of the great striker Giorgio Chinaglia. In the 1980s they spent six years in Serie B, much to the joy of their bitter cross-town rivals, Roma. But they have gotten progressively more competitive in the last decade and since 1993 have always finished in the top five.

Lazio's rise peaked during one week at the end of February, when they beat Juventus 1−0 in Turin in the Italian Cup, and dominated Inter at home, 3−0, in the league. Some people besides Lazio fans suddenly started taking the club seriously. Croatian attacker Alen Boksic finally came to life after five years in Italy, and Eriksson convinced playmaker Roberto Mancini to join him in Rome after fifteen years at Sampdoria, in Genova. 'I've coached him for six years now, and each year he just keeps getting better,' Eriksson said of Mancini, a spunky 33-year-old. Although he has never had much luck on the national squad, Mancini consistently proves that he fits the description for what Italians call a *trascinatore*, which literally means swayer, but in reality is football's version of the Terminator, the guy who can make and break games.

Lazio's offensive strike also included Pierluigi Casiraghi, a powerful, towering attacker who humiliated Inter in their February match. But Boksic—Mancini—Casiraghi meant there was no room on the pitch for Giuseppe Signori, a tiny but effective striker who scored 26 goals in 1993, 23 the following season, and 24 in 1995–96. Signori, one of the favourites at Stadio Olimpico and captain of the team, didn't feel like sitting on the bench, and was put on loan to Sampdoria at the end of November.

In hindsight, it was a mistake for Signori to leave. In 12 games at Sampdoria he had scored just 3 goals, and was already being booed by the fans. He may not have been a starter at Lazio, but with the team heading for the Final of the Italian Cup, he would have seen some playing time. Casiraghi later spent considerable periods of each game on the sidelines as well, as Lazio decided to go with the simple dual attack of Boksic and Mancini.

Roma play a 4–3–3 and are one of the most exciting teams to watch in Serie A for their speed. Once they get control of the ball in midfield the forwards start cutting diagonally through the opposing defence, and the crowd at Stadio Olimpico erupts with joy at the mere possibility of some goal action. They were level for the most goals scored during the season, 67, with 1st-place Juventus, but their three-pronged attack also left them unprotected at times at the back, and Roma conceded 42 goals, compared to 28 for Juventus.

Lazio, on the other hand, take to the field with the more conservative 4–4–2, and don't, as a rule, attack with the same intensity as Roma. Alen Boksic is their real striker, and Roberto Mancini plays a little behind him. But they have two midfielders who were also very offensively minded, Pavel Nedved, who finished the season with 11 goals, and Diego Fuser, who scored 8.

In a word, Roma concentrate on scoring goals; Lazio – until they broke down at the end of the season – spent most of the year preventing them, but still scored when they needed to.

Udinese, who have been in Serie A for most of the nineties, while not quite as impressive as Lazio, also surprised people this season. German striker Oliver Bierhoff led the 'top cannon' competition with 17 goals after 22 games. Gabriel Batistuta of Fiorentina and Alessandro Del Piero of Juventus each had 15 tallies, and Ronaldo was trailing with 14. Bierhoff had a remarkable year, and it was he who handed Inter their first loss with a goal in injury time before a delirious crowd in December. The wealthier squads were already lining up to buy the German forward. The smart money put him with either Milan or Juventus. Financially, Italian football is still really a three-team league, with Inter, Juve and Milan in a class by themselves.

In Parma's thrashing of Udinese, Lilian Thuram had shut down Bierhoff, and that was that. The Brazilian Amoroso and Paolo Poggi occasionally threatened, but Parma were in control. The return leg was more complicated. Although Ancelotti's boys took an early lead with a goal by Crespo, Thuram picked up two yellow cards for his close marking of the German bomber and was sent off before the end of the first half. Parma tried to hold on with ten men, but 10 minutes from the finish Udinese equalized. Bierhoff, of course.

Bierhoff wasn't the only person at Udinese who was being courted by other squads. Coach Alberto Zaccheroni, 44, whose contract expired in June, was also in the running for a bigger and better job – not to mention a salary increase that would probably double the 600 million lire (roughly £210,000) he was currently making. Rumours had Zaccheroni at either Inter or Real Madrid, although there was also an outside chance he could go to Parma.

Udinese also play the 4–3–3. Their success is largely due to their coach, Alberto Zaccheroni, and to some very smart buying. They are renowned for their agressive scouting and recruiting, but

57

they pick up only those players they can afford. Although the club paid 6 billion lire (more than £2 million) for Amoroso, Bierhoff was picked up for the next to nothing from a squad in Serie B, Ascoli – where he wasn't even scoring that much (9 goals in 33 games) – while two Danish players (including World Cup star Thomas Helveg) and an Egyptian (Hazem Emam) combined didn't cost $1 million. For a dozen foreigners they paid 20 billion lire (£7 million), or about what Parma paid for one Italian striker, Enrico Chiesa. The problem was that by March Bierhoff had 17 goals while Chiesa was still stuck with 7.

Udinese and Lazio weren't the only threats to the Inter-Milan-Juve triumvirate. Fiorentina were also doing their best to keep Serie A from becoming the exclusive domain of the Milan-Turin axis. Florence may be a small and tranquil Tuscan city, but Fiorentina's owner has an ego and bank account that are both healthy enough to challenge the big guys. Vittorio Cecchi Gori, a sort of 'Berlusconi Junior', makes his millions producing films, and has a virtual stranglehold on production and distribution in Italy. Florentines are known for being frank and direct, and Cecchi Gori remains true to his roots. When Fiorentina weren't playing particularly well against Parma in December, Cecchi Gori burst into the dressing room and threatened to fire the first-year coach, Alberto Malesani. He finally calmed down and Malesani, who was defended by his squad, kept his job. At least for the time being.

That was probably all for the best. At 43 Malesani may still be young and inexperienced as a Serie A coach, but after 22 matches Fiorentina were level in 5th place with Parma and Roma. And on the same day that Lazio blanked Inter 3–0, Fiorentina shut out Juventus by the same score. Up until then Malesani was among the lowest-paid coaches in the first division, making about 500 million lire (£175,000) a year.

Whatever he gets paid, the young coach earns it in putting up with the pressure. While the stress and strains are intense on any team in Serie A, some owners are more difficult than others, and Cecchi Gori would rank among the most difficult. He's fiery and unpredictable, and Malesani's making it past mid-season already showed that he was a survivor. He had a difficult situation to manage, with some temperamental players, and for a while it looked like star Argentinian striker Gabriel Batistuta was on his way to Inter. After Malesani nearly lost his job, Batistuta gave an interview to a local radio station in which his criticism of Cecchi Gori wasn't so muted: 'It will be difficult for Fiorentina to become a great club if halfway through a game the coach is threatened with being sacked because he's not winning against Parma.'

Fiorentina made a big splash when they called in their boy from Brazil, Edmundo, early into the new year. Fiorentina paid some 12 billion lire (£4 million) to Vasco da Gama for even more offensive punch. But by mid-February Edmundo, nicknamed 'the Animal', was already unhappy because he wasn't used to bench-warming. He got on a plane and went home to celebrate Carnival in Rio de Janeiro, and said he didn't plan on returning to Italy. 'Here in Brazil I'll always be a starter,' he said. But Edmundo's absence from the Italian league championship didn't seem to matter much for Malesani's squad; they went out and humiliated 1st-place Juventus with three unanswered goals by Aldo Firicano, A.L. Oliveira, and Anselmo Robbiati. That would be enough to keep Cecchi Gori calm for a week or so.

Fiorentina proved especially dangerous when playing at home. They have a small stadium and extremely rambunctious fans, who celebrate the start of every game with a kind of fireworks show. The supporters frequently manage to spook other clubs into a state of total nervousness. Fortunately, there's a tall plexiglass wall protecting players from outraged fans, who love to mock anyone they don't happen to like, which means just about everybody else.

Young kids, no more than 10 or 12 years old, pounded the plexiglass behind Ancelotti, attempting to rattle him when Parma played at Florence in December. Roberto Baggio remains a favourite target, since he became famous with Fiorentina but then deserted Tuscany for the big time (and big money) at the much-hated Juventus. In Florence, they haven't forgotten.

They have come up with a replacement bomber, Batistuta, who

59

has been in the top of class scorers. Teamed up with Domenico Morfeo and Oliveira, Batistuta has produced both goals and excitement for the 'Viola' or violet squad. They have a strong international midfield, with Robbiati, the Russian Andrej Kanchelskis, Swede Stefan Schwarz and Portuguese standout Manuel Rui Costa.

Although they have a very competent young keeper, Francesco Toldo, it was their leaky defence that kept Fiorentina from the top of the rankings. They had failed to learn the first rule of Serie A: don't concede any goals, or at least never more than one a game. After 27 regular season matches they had scored 51 goals (more than any other teams bar Juventus and Inter), but let in 29. Fiorentina have only won the *scudetto* twice in their history, in 1956 and 1969, and they weren't going to get it this season either, no matter how much Cecchi Gori shouted.

Roma, like dreaded rival Lazio, enjoy the support of some of the most fervent fans in Serie A. But 'the Wolves' have won the *scudetto* in only two seasons, and one of those was more than fifty years ago. Ancelotti was on the 1983 championship team, a side which had a great midfield, including the Brazilian Paulo Roberto Falcao and Herbert Prohaska, now coach of Austria, and was led by Bruno Conti in attack. Ancelotti also won the Italian Cup with Roma in 1984 and 1986. And in 1984, of course, they made it to the Final of the European Cup against Liverpool, and although they had the home advantage they could only manage a 1–1 draw, and lost the Cup on penalty kicks.

The Wolves have not been lucky. They should have won the *scudetto* in 1986 (when Ericksson was the manager) but in the second-last game of the season, playing at home, they lost to last-place Lecce 2–3. Roma fans have grown accustomed to heartbreak. This season they played well, if not exceptionally. Argentine striker Abel Balbo had 13 goals after 22 games, and Francesco Totti, a home-grown 22-year-old forward, showed occasional streaks of glory. Not enough to get called to the World Cup in Paris, but he's still young. Roma were playing a lot like Parma, if not in style at least in the results they were obtaining, and were level in

5th place with Ancelotti's squad early into the second half of the season.

Throughout most of the season Roma played well when they had their Brazilians – Aldair and Cafu in defence, Paulo Sergio in attack – and noticeably poorer when they were missing for their national team matches and Nike tournaments. Austrian keeper Michael Konsel saved several games for Roma, including the one against Parma. But as the season wore on, Roma looked like they were on their way to yet another respectable – but not great – year. Typical Roma.

The *giallorossi* have one of the most enigmatic and phlegmatic coaches in Serie A in Zdenek Zeman. A chain smoker, the 50-year-old Czech has a deep, gravelly voice, but hardly ever uses it. While other coaches will stand, wave, run and yell to encourage or correct their boys, Zeman sits in silence. And smokes. He hides his sense of humour away deeply, and only brings it out on special occasions. Once, when he was manager at Lazio, he did take part in a nice April Fool's trick. He gave an interview to a local radio station early in the morning and explained, with no emotion what-soever (which he's very good at), why they had sold their top scorer, Giuseppe Signori.

A former volleyball player known as 'the Bohemian' (he escaped from Czechoslovakia in 1968), Zeman placed his name on the Italian football map when he put together a winning squad in the southern town of Foggia in the early 1990s. He first brought the team from Serie B to A, and then managed to keep it in the first division for the three years he was there – no easy task with a team from the south that isn't known for its deep pockets.

From Foggia Zeman jumped up to Lazio, where he led the Eagles to 2nd- and 3rd-place finishes before being fired in his third season. For someone who was replaced mid-season, Zeman made out all right financially. His contract with Roma gave him close to $1 million (£600,000) a year, and placed him among the better paid coaches in Serie A. Fabio Capello at Milan and Marcello Lippi at Juventus were perhaps paid a little more than Zeman; Ancelotti was not very far behind. Zeman, whose contract with

Roma was renewed during the season, actually had a brief affair with Parma, ten years earlier. But it lasted for just seven games. After four losses, two draws and a win, Zeman was out looking for another job.

Among the new competitors, Lazio have the best chance of bringing home the *scudetto*. Udinese have lost their manager, Alberto Zaccheroni, and two of the main cogs in the machine: bomber Oliver Bierhoff and midfielder Thomas Helveg will join the 'Zack Attack' at Milan. Fiorentina have hired Giovanni Trapattoni, but at the time of writing management were still fighting with Gabriel Batistuta, who wanted to leave. Lazio has sold Josh Chamot and Vladimir Jugovic to Atlético Madrid, and will be missing Alessandro Nesta for the first part of the season, since the young defender was injured at the World Cup. But they have new additions, including Chilean attacker Marcelo Salas, and the Yugoslavian midfielder Dejan Stankovic. And, above all, owner Sergio Cragnotti has money to spend.

5 The Usual Suspects: Inter, Juve, Milan

When Massimo Moratti bought Inter in 1995, Milan owner Silvio Berlusconi warned him about spending too much money going after players. 'You start out wisely and then you see the possibilities and you start wasting money,' Berlusconi admonished his new competitor. Moratti assured his rival owner he wouldn't fall into that trap. And Moratti doesn't look like someone who would gamble too often. With his tailor-made charcoal suits and his calm demeanour, he carries his name with dignity. Moratti belongs to a genteel, educated caste known as *Milano bene*. Their money is old, their wine is old, their homes are ancient.

But three years and a hundred million pounds after the purchase, it's clear that Berlusconi was right. 'It happens,' Moratti said, with a shrug. Berlusconi knows better than most, and should have heeded his own advice. Milan spent more than £17 million on this season's squad, and still couldn't win. Both teams wanted Ronaldo, but Moratti admitted that his move was, above all, aggressive defence. (Lazio were also hot for Ronaldo, but had to settle for the Chilean attacker Marcelo 'El Matador' Salas, whom they bought a year later from River Plate for 37.5 billion lire, roughly £13 million.)

'We first got into the negotiations for Ronaldo to keep the others from getting him,' Moratti said. 'But then once we were in the heat of the battle we didn't want to let go.' The official price tag for the transfer from Barcelona was 50 billion lire, not counting Ronaldo's salary. (The transfer fee was more than three times what Inter got from Arsenal for Dennis Bergkamp.) Berlusconi later claimed that Ronaldo was too expensive, since the overall cost, including a nine-year contract, was around 100 billion lire. Fiat chief Gianni Agnelli, whose family owns Juventus, acknowledged Ronaldo's football skills, but cast doubt about him as a wise investment.

Moratti saw Ronaldo slump in mid-season (he went six games without a goal as Inter slipped into 2nd place behind Juve) and publicly criticized the play of the Brazilian. But he never doubted that his landing football's brightest star was the deal of the decade. 'All told, he was the player who cost me the least,' the owner said. Ronaldo may pick up a hefty cheque at the end of every month (his yearly pay from Inter is estimated at 7.2 billion lire or £2.5 million) but he also brings in fans, season-ticket holders, sponsors, and, Moratti hopes, victories. Inter took in more than £13 million in stadium receipts this season. A 1st- or 2nd-place finish means qualification for the Champions League, and that means television rights and money for a squad — as much as £10 million if a team makes it to the Final. In addition, after bringing in Ronaldo Inter signed an eleven-year contract with Nike, worth 220 billion lire (more than £75 million).

With the kind of money the top Italian teams dish out, winning is no longer simply an option. It's do or die. Roy Hodgson brought Inter to 3rd place in the standings behind Juventus and Parma in the 1996–97 season, and made it to the Final of the UEFA Cup, where they lost on penalty kicks, but that wasn't good enough. Hodgson was battling with the press and the fans, and took an offer from Blackburn Rovers when it came along. Moratti called Hodgson an educated and capable coach, but regretted seeing the Mister challenge the press and the fans. 'Unfortunately that doesn't help you win the consensus of either the press or the fans,' the owner said. Hodgson came to Moratti one day at the end of the season and told him he had received a good offer. 'I imagine that you're happy,' Hodgson told Moratti, to which the owner replied, 'Not at all, but I think it's the most intelligent thing.'

Moratti comes from the very cream of Milanese high society,

but he's held in thrall by the labourers, shopkeepers and cab drivers who fill his stadium every two weeks. '*Il pubblico*,' as he calls the fans, 'absolutely have got to be listened to and respected. Your public is like a big animal with instincts that are a lot quicker than those of any single person with the team. So if they give a sign, even if it seems out of place, you've got to know how to pick up on it. The best things about football are two-fold: the public and the players.'

Football fans may seem like a bunch of hoods to the rest of *Milano bene* (and Inter has its share of violent animals in the *curva*) but Moratti sees a side in them that's almost maternal. 'I've often seen games where Inter were not playing badly, but nevertheless the reaction from the fans was silence,' he noted. 'And right after that we took a goal. The public has these incredible sensors in which they can pick up certain sensations before everybody else, like a mother with her child. They know when the child's in danger.'

The owner treats his players with great respect, and before acquiring Ronaldo he asked Djorkaeff's opinion about the deal. 'Youri's a champion in his own right, and he's French; they're sensitive about these things.' Djorkaeff had no doubts that it was the right move, even if it meant that he would be taking a step back, both on the field and off it. 'Together we'll tear them apart,' he told Moratti. And for most of the season they did. They led the league until the very last game of the first half of the season, when they drew with Empoli and Juventus won, pushing the black and whites up by a point. They would later have a chance to overtake Juve when they faced off directly, but they lost what would become the most talked about match of the season.

Moratti admitted that he bought Inter for sentimental reasons. He called it a *debolezza*, or weakness. It was one that cost him about £25 million. 'It's true that because of the risk, I didn't have the support of those who are close to me. But it was one of those things that you know you should do.' He brushed aside reports that his wife Milly was against the investment, and that she wanted to spend the money in some way that was more socially useful.

Moratti smiled and said that wasn't true, or not completely true, in any case: 'In the end football does a lot to help society; it makes people happy.'

AC Milan were the Italian team of the early 1990s, winning the *scudetto* four out of five seasons from 1991 to 1996. But after a 1st-place finish in the '95–96 season, coach Fabio Capello departed for Madrid and the Devils finished an embarassing 11th the following year. A Milan cycle had come to an end, and despite Capello's return, they only managed to finish 10th in 1998. 'It's like the Chicago Bulls,' said Lanfranco Vaccari of *La Gazzetta dello Sport*. 'Once they lose Jordan, Pippen and Rodman they won't win again for another fifteen years. Milan were a squad in need of being re-made, but Berlusconi and [managing director Adriano] Galliani had the idea that their team was eternal. There's something infantile about it.'

The great central defender Franco Baresi played until the end of the 1996–97 season, at which point he had already turned 37. Then when their crisis began this season they recalled an old stalwart, Roberto Donadoni, who was already well on his way to his 35th birthday and had gone off to play in the United States. And even after a terribly disappointing season, they didn't seem to get it, and went chasing 30-year-old Oliver Bierhoff. A great bomber, but an ageing one who would only be good for a year or two, and not the kind of player who's going to help you start a new cycle.

Despite their dominance in the early part of the decade, the squad has been debt heavy, and their post-Bosman tactic was to take players who were free agents, so they wouldn't have to pay the teams anything for breaking a contract. 'Who do you get as a free agent?' Vaccari asked. 'Four losers from Holland? Kluivert is a great player for France, or Holland, where there are two great teams. But here in Italy it's another game.' Kluivert proved to be Milan's greatest disappointment, but he was only one among many. There was also Ibrahim Ba of France, the Brazilian Leonardo, and Winston Bogarde of Holland. Even the old stalwarts didn't look the same, especially Sebastiano Rossi in goal, and Paolo Maldini and Alessandro Costacurta in defence.

Milan's malaise was attributed to what the analysts call 'the end of a cycle'. It is taken for granted that a great team eventually ages and can't dominate for more than a few years. The Milan of Sacchi and Capello relied on only three foreigners, all Dutch (Rikaard, Van Basten, and Gullit), while the '97–98 Milan saw sixteen different non-Italians from ten different nations on the field.

There was plenty of energy, but no synergy. How else to explain that Patrick Kluivert couldn't buy a goal at Milan, and then led Holland into the semi-finals of the World Cup? Or that Capello kept Edgar Davids on the bench, but then the midfielder became a cornerstone of both the Juve and the Dutch national teams?

Dutch defender Winston Bogarde, who made a stupid back pass that lost a game for Milan early on, was sent to Barcelona way back in November; whereas after the season Marcel Desailly had been sold to Chelsea. Croatian Dario Smoje was off to Serie B at Monza, while keeper Massimo Taibi, an occasional starter, would start the next season at Venezia, newly promoted in A. Dejan Savicevic, Filippo Maniero, Patrick Kluivert and the Brazilian Cruz were also all up for sale.

Nothing seemed to go right for Milan at the beginning of the season. The nadir arrived on October 19, when they lost 1–2 at home to last-place Lecce. The cellar dwellers had lost every game so far during the season, yet sneaked out of enemy territory with a victory against some of the best names in football today. It didn't seem to matter that Milan fielded two extraordinarily powerful strikers, Liberian George Weah and Dutchman Patrick Kluivert, and high-priced midfielders Ibrahim Ba and Leonardo. The only goal Milan scored came when a Lecce defender put the ball into his own net.

Milan have taken advantage of the Bosman ruling, which puts no limits on the number of European Community players on a team, but to the point of exaggeration. At one point against Lecce only three of the eleven players on the field were Italian. The Tower of Babel effect may have been part of the problem, although brilliant footballers should be able to play together even if they don't speak the same language. Brazilian star Ronaldo didn't have a command of Italian at the beginning of the season, but still manages to score plenty of goals for cross-town rival Internazionale.

Perhaps Berlusconi bought the wrong goods. 'Everything that looked like it was top-of-the-line probably wasn't top-of-the-line,' said Gianni Rivera, who starred for Milan in the 1960s. 'I don't think the difficulty is necessarily too many foreigners. If every one of them was an outstanding player, it wouldn't be a problem.' But Milan fan Andrea Bettetini pointed out that when Milan were at their peak in the early 1990s they had a good mix of foreign stars, including three Dutchmen, and local talent from the Lombardy region, who had grown up with the club. 'For the guys who are there now, it's all the same whether they're playing for Barcelona or Milan or Paris Saint-Germain,' noted Bettetini.

The humiliation of Milan was especially painful this year because perennial rivals Inter were at the top of the standings, more than ten places up the table. Berlusconi may have spent more than $17 million on eleven players, or an entire squad, while Inter president Massimo Moratti gambled more than that on Ronaldo alone, but Moratti's risk-taking appeared to have paid off, at least in the rivalry with Milan.

Italian fans found it strange to see Milan *mezzaclassifica*. This was the squad that under Arrigo Sacchi changed Italian football. 'Italian teams used to try to sneak by their opponents,' Ancelotti said. 'They weren't trying to show that they were better; they were trying to show that they were shrewder. Sacchi changed that. The teams took the pitch to win, to dominate the other squad.' No more cheap goals and then lock-up defence, or playing for the draw in away games. Sacchi wanted intense, aggressive play, always aimed for victory.

It was the kind of football that owner Silvio Berlusconi liked – exciting, powerful and dominating. So no one was the least bit surprised to see that when he entered politics in 1994 Berlusconi played on Milan's success and used football imagery, even in the name of his party. 'Forza Italia' was the cheer supporters used for the national team. (Most have since stopped, to avoid any possible misunderstanding.) 'I'm taking the field,' Berlusconi announced when he entered the political ring for the first time. 'And I play to win.' Unfortunately for the millionaire media magnate, he's enjoyed more wins on the pitch than in politics. Forza Italia did well in its first try at the polls, and Berlusconi was named Prime Minister, but he was forced to resign seven months later when his coalition fell apart.

6 February

Parma v Bari
February 1 1998

In theory, you really shouldn't have to get too uptight about an opponent whose best season in Serie A saw them finish in 7th place, especially when that was fifty years ago. Bari are a team that would like to be in the first division, although they can't seem to stay there. But anything can happen on any Sunday in Italian football, and it was Bari that handed Inter their second loss of the season the previous week, allowing Juventus to move to the top of Serie A. And the squad's mid-table standing was hardly indicative of their capabilities, or their modest past, which includes a 1990 Mitropa Cup (whatever that is) and a 1981 Italian Cup for their junior team.

Although they had beaten Bari in the first game of the season, back in August, and twice in Italian Cup competitions, Parma took their opponents very seriously. Bari were capable of surprises. As they showed when striker Gian Luca Zambrotta hit the crossbar 7 minutes into the game. They were not often a threat (they had only two shots on goal) but they were often in control, and the first half ended 0–0. Parma fans were not happy and on several occasions whistled their displeasure. Faustino Asprilla, not yet ready to make his debut, watched from the stands. Hernán Crespo was also in the stands, since Ancelotti had decided to start the tiny Brazilian Bolzan Adailton in his place.

For all of their struggles, Bari still had a handful of talented players, including the Moroccan defender Rachid Negrouz, Swedish midfielder Klas Ingesson, and striker Phil Masinga, a South

African. Negrouz earned a rather dubious distinction for himself earlier in the season when he began pinching the butts of opposing attackers to throw them off. To a certain degree it worked. Juventus' Filippo Inzaghi was clearly rattled by such unexpected affection. Negrouz marked Adailton in the game against Parma, and the Brazilian had no complaints, so perhaps Negrouz had learned to keep his hands to himself.

Neither Adailton nor his striking partner, Enrico Chiesa, managed to penetrate the Bari defence very effectively. Bari played an offside trap, and Parma got caught in it eight times. Negrouz took control of Adailton; Luigi Sala marked Chiesa. But the real problem was, again, in midfield. Bari effectively closed up all the open spaces, preventing Parma from moving the ball around and forcing them to try to hit attackers with long passes. With the exception of Dino Baggio, the entire midfield looked like it was *sotto-tono*, or out of shape. Nestor Sensini, back from injury, was still not in top form, and neither Stefano Fiore nor Mario Stanic on the wings looked sharp. Ancelotti couldn't be happy about much in the first half, perhaps only that they weren't playing Juventus or Inter. The defence, with veteran Luigi Apolloni in the place of Fabio Cannavaro (sprained ankle), was solid but not brilliant. After Bari hit the crossbar early in the game, goalkeeper Buffon was never tested.

Early in the second half Ancelotti sent Blomqvist on for Fiore, and the Swede played well, creating several dangerous occasions for Parma. But the home team didn't get on the scoreboard until the 68th minute, when they pulled off a textbook counter-attack of fine passing and hustle. Dino Baggio stole the ball from Negrouz, who was approaching midfield, and pushed it out on the right to Enrico Chiesa. The attacker took two steps and saw Stanic wide open across the field. In a beautiful show of precision he placed the ball on the head of the Croat, who dropped it at the feet of a sprinting Baggio, now alone in front of the keeper. Baggio picked up his fifth goal of the season, which was not bad for a midfielder known more for his defensive capabilities than his scoring. Strikers Crespo and Chiesa each had only six.

Parma had a chance to make it 2–0 when Chiesa crossed to Stanic in front of the goal, but Stanic headed it high over the crossbar. So the game ended in classic Parma fashion: a typical performance, a typical result – 1–0. They don't seem to care if they don't score a lot of goals as long as they don't give up any. Ancelotti was not ecstatic after the game – he couldn't be after a disappointing January – but he was happy about the three points. Lazio hit the post twice but failed to beat Napoli, so Parma and Lazio were level in 4th place with 32 points. Juve and Inter both won, and Juventus kept a one-point lead at the top, 41 to 40. Udinese lost at Fiorentina and were now 3rd with 34.

After victories, Ancelotti becomes a different person. He's got those three points in his pocket, and nobody can take them away. Even if they didn't gain any ground on Juve or Inter, they didn't lose any either. The victory over Bari was important precisely because they were expected to win, and because they had played so poorly in losing to Brescia and Sampdoria the previous month.

'We're up and down; this isn't the Parma I like,' Ancelotti said. 'We've got to find that consistency we've had in the past. In the first half we were blocked, psychologically. In the second half it went a little better. It's a delicate time during the season. This victory lets us work with a little more tranquillity.' Ancelotti promised that Parma would start playing better, and he seemed to believe it too. He insisted he wasn't just playing mind games.

Ancelotti, who was dressed for the game in a classic blue suit, didn't worry too much about how it matched with his baseball hat, a gift from the hard-core fans known as the 'Boys'. This is one of his good luck charms, and he wears it from start to finish of every game. He took it off only once against Bari, when the referee came over to ask him to tone down his protests. 'A sign of respect,' the Mister explained later.

'About 99 per cent of the people in this business are superstitious, and I'm not part of the one per cent,' Parma's Mister once remarked. And yet, Ancelotti doesn't make too much of his lucky charms. He's serious about the Catholic faith he grew up with, and attends an anticipated Sunday mass, on Saturday evening, every week that Parma plays at home.

Atalanta v Parma
February 8 1998

While this was technically a home game for Atalanta, it was not played at the squad's stadium in Bergamo. The league imposed a sanction on the team for its fans' behaviour during an Italian Cup game against Parma, when both the referee and the 'fourth man' were pelted with coins. So the game was played at Cremona, a neutral site not far from Milan. When the two teams had met at the beginning of the season, Parma let a victory slip away. They were down 1–0 then scored two goals to take the lead. But it was Cristiano Lucarelli's day, and the Atalanta striker scored his second goal of the game 20 minutes into the second half to even the score.

There was no victory to let slip away at Cremona, and the match ended 0–0, the only game of the day not to see a goal (Empoli pounded Napoli 5–0 and Udinese humiliated Lecce 6–0). Cremona is the hometown of Enrico Chiesa, but that connection was of little use to Parma's attacker. There were no special vibes on the pitch for Enrico, who hardly ever saw a ball. Although the field was neutral, the game was not. Parma were outplayed by a team that was fourth from the bottom of Serie A, and fighting to avoid relegation. Parma couldn't construct anything, especially in the first half, and were again forced to try to reach Chiesa and Crespo with long passes. The long-ball didn't work either. Dino Baggio pulled a muscle early on and was replaced in midfield by Federico Giunti.

Atalanta pressed frequently, and Buffon made a couple of stellar saves, but it was not great football. Although Parma had a couple of good chances to score, Crespo shooting just wide on one, they finished with just two shots on goal to Atalanta's four. More telling were the corner kicks: Atalanta had eleven to Parma's four.

Although they had the chance to score, Ancelotti admitted that his squad would not have merited the victory had they slipped one in. The only positive aspect he could find was the defence. While not perfect, they did manage to keep their opponents from scoring.

Parma needed the three points from a victory to stay even with Lazio, who played spectacularly in a 2–1 victory over Milan at home. This was Lazio's sixth victory in eight games and pushed them into 4th place behind Juve, Inter and Udinese.

7 The Tifoso: Football Fever

Andrea Pelosio, a 36-year-old geologist, followed two teams as a kid. He rooted for Internazionale in Serie A, as well as his hometown squad of Parma, then in Serie C. That changed when Parma moved into Serie A, and Pelosio decided he would follow only the *gialloblu*. A former player, who would have gotten a call from Bologna as a keeper had he not been injured in a motorcycle accident, Pelosio has enjoyed watching Parma's success. But the 1997–98 squad was not his idea of good football, and he laid the blame largely on Carlo Ancelotti.

'He doesn't have the experience for a squad that wants to win in A,' Pelosio argued. 'He took Reggiana from B to A, but that's a much different championship.' Pelosio won't even give Ancelotti much credit for bringing Parma into 2nd place in his first season. 'Last year was a lot less complicated,' he said. 'Lazio were the only team in competition with us for second place. Now there are at least four other teams as strong as Parma.' Or maybe five or six.

Parma were missing the *fantasista*, the director of operations, who makes the last pass or next-to-last pass and pushes the play forward, Pelosio insisted. 'He sent Zola away because Zola doesn't fit into his kind of football. [Midfielder Pietro] Strada was the only one with a little bit of fantasy, and he got hurt early in the season.' Much of what Pelosio said was reasonable, but he pushed it more than a bit when he claimed Parma would be in 1st or 2nd place if Nevio Scala were still running the show.

That was Monday morning coaching, and could never even be tested, but he persisted. 'Look at the players they've bought: Crespo, Chiesa, Stanic. Scala didn't have guys of that calibre, or with those pricetags.' Pelosio complained that Ancelotti is true to his roots: obstinate. (People from Parma call anyone from Reggiana, such as Ancelotti, a *testa quadra*, or square head.) Ancelotti's refusal to go from a traditional 4–4–2 configuration to a more dynamic and offensive-minded 3–4–3 had Pelosio convinced that Parma's Mister was living in the past. 'Last year they had one of the strongest defences in the league, and Ancelotti doesn't want to let that go.'

On that point, at least, Ancelotti would agree. Actually, Parma had the second-best defence in 1996–97; champions Juventus were first on defence as well, once again proof that the team that allows the fewest goals normally wins the *scudetto*. 'I spend a lot more time working on what the team should be doing when we don't have possession of the ball than what we do when we do have possession,' Ancelotti conceded. But he didn't agree that it was time for everyone to play a 3–4–3. 'That all depends on the players you have,' he said. 'And then, the difference between a 4–4–2 and 3–4–3 can be seen a lot better in theory than in practice. If you look at Parma on the field it almost never looks like a 4–4–2, because players are continually moving up and down the field.'

Pelosio echoed the feelings of many observers of Parma when he pointed out that the midfield hardly ever manages to get any good balls to the strikers. 'The other night (Filippo) Inzaghi scored two goals for Juventus, but he probably had ten chances,' Pelosio complains. 'For us, Crespo might get two good balls a game. OK, so he misses one of the goals. But you have to have a few more chances.'

Pelosio pointed out that as a player, Ancelotti was never captain of the team. 'He wasn't a leader when he played and he still doesn't have that ability to inspire the kids on the team.' That may be true, but very few coaches in A do have the magic wand that holds their young charges in thrall.

Even the best Italian coaches have had rocky relations with their teams. Capello was considered one of the best misters around after winning championships in Italy and Spain, but struggled when he came back to Milan. The situation exacerbated to such a point that by the end of the season he was criticizing captain Paolo

Maldini, a mini-legend at Milan, in front of the other players. And Giovanni Trapattoni, who took up the offer to manage Franz Beckenbauer's Bayern Munich, left after quarrelling with some of his better players.

None of the coaches currently in A had a career as a player as brilliant as Carlo Ancelotti. Most of them, including Marcello Lippi of Juventus, Fabio Capello of Milan, and Gigi Simoni of Inter were nothing exceptional as players. Alberto Malesani of Fiorentina barely made it into Serie C as a midfielder. Giovanni Trapattoni was the exception: a very good player (he once shut down Pelé) who turned into a great coach.

Pelosio believes Parma fans were spoiled by their very success, four Cups in four years: the Italian Cup in 1992; Cup Winners' Cup in 1993; European Super Cup in 1994, and the UEFA Cup in 1995. 'We won so much so early that the fans became accustomed to it,' Pelosio notes.

Pelosio may believe Parma's biggest lacuna was a midfielder who organized the attack. But he also admitted that there was also a question of luck. 'You know the difference between Inter and Parma?' he asked. 'Inter won a bunch of games this year in the 95th minute, already in injury time. Parma lost them in the 95th minute.'

Maurizio Serio has two teams in Serie A, Bari and Juventus. Bari because he's from Bari, Juventus 'because when I reached the age of reason this was the great Juve of Michel Platini'. Serio is used to being disappointed by Bari, but still manages to see every game. 'As soon as they find someone who's really good, they sell him, so of course the fans get angry,' he says. But he loves the Mister, Eugenio Fascetti. 'Somebody who goes out to the journalists and tells them, "You guys are busting my balls" – now that's a coach.'

Fascetti actually chased one particular ballbuster journalist around a practice field. The Mister has developed a squad that plays a tight man-to-man defence (better for Negrouz to get inside their pants) but has no attack. Phil Masinga runs like mad and was a bomber in South Africa, but would finish the season with only

77

nine goals. A promising young attacker, Nicola Ventola, went out with a knee injury at the beginning of the season, and that did considerable harm to Bari's year.

Bari could never fathom a *scudetto*, not even in their wildest dreams. They live for two things: to avoid relegation and finish above archrival Lecce, a town just to the south of Bari. 'All the team has to do is win the derby with Lecce and they've got the fans with them,' Serio says. He regards it 'a great season' if the squad manages to finish 10th. And that normally means topping Lecce at the same time. The *Baresi* frequently find themselves on the verge of relegation, which means staying in Serie A is cause for fireworks and major festivities. Literally. Like most southern Italians, the *Baresi* like fireworks.

Bari have the most beautiful stadium in Serie A, which might seem strange since the team spends nearly as much time in B as it does in A. But, no matter. The white bowl-like structure was built for the World Cup in 1990. Designed by Renzo Piano of Genova, Italy's top architect, who also designed the Osaka airport and (with Richard Rogers) the Pompidou Centre in Paris, it's a nice little showpiece for Bari.

A nice big showpiece, actually, given that it can seat 60,000. The city is the home of the Mattarrese family, also known as the Kennedys of Bari. One brother, Antonio Mattarrese, is the former head of the Italian football federation, the FIGC; another is a bishop, which means a lot in Catholic Italy; and a third, Vincenzo, runs the Bari team and works in the family construction business.

Bari, a bustling southern port city, is known for great seafood, a deep-dish pizza called focaccia, and scores of pickpockets and purse snatchers in the old part of the city. The Cathedral of Bari, which dates from twelfth century, holds the mortal remains of St Nicholas, from whom we have conjured up Santa Claus. The stadium, like dozens of other establishments in the city, including the Sheraton Hotel, is named after San Nicola. This is Bari's patron saint, and when the city held a referendum to decide the name of the new field, 'San Nicola' crushed the runner-up, which was 'Mediterraneo'.

The most beautiful stadium in the country, yes, but not the best place to see a game. Like the stadium Juventus use in Turin, Lo Stadio delle Alpe, there's a track separating the field from the stands. Juve may be the most popular team in the country, and perhaps the world, but the Stadio delle Alpe is only half full for most matches, largely because the Juventus fanbase is so widely spread, the stadium offers poor views, and it's expensive to buy a ticket. At Bari, they only manage to fill the stadium, which can seat 58,000, at the biggest games: Juventus, Milan and Inter. 'You can't see the field very well and if there's wind you freeze,' said Serio. 'You can see something from above, but not much from below, and nothing at all from the *curva*. Renzo Piano, the guy who built it, is a great architect, but if you sit there on a cold and windy day you're going to get pneumonia.'

Although they like to stay in Serie A, what Bari fans want most is hustle, heart and real play. 'We lost 5–1 with Juventus once, but played well,' Serio said. 'That's all right. The problem is when you pay the price of admission and they don't give you anything for it. They lose 1–0 or 2–0 but play badly. Fans don't like being jerked around. So it becomes a kind of love-hate relationship.'

The only Serie A games broadcast live are done through satellite, and fans can only see the away games. Illegally, you can use low-frequency contraptions that can pick up the local games, and Bari is full of them. Not surprisingly, even inmates at the Bari prison see the home team in an effort to catch what Serio calls *emozioni forti*, or strong feelings. 'The problem isn't whether we stay in A or drop into B; it's whether or not they give us *emozioni forti*. A couple of years ago, when Igor Protti scored 22 goals, that was an *emozione forte*.'

Marco Calvani, 33, has lived in Rome nearly all of his life, and loves football. But he refuses to go to see either of the Serie A teams, Lazio or Roma, who play at the giant Stadio Olimpico. Instead, the lawyer goes with several of his friends each Saturday afternoon to see Lodigiani, who are in Serie C1 and play at the tiny Stadio Flaminio. 'We get the best seats in the house for 20,000 lire (£7) and it's nice and peaceful,' he said. 'We like it because it's the kind of football that's closer to us. There aren't a bunch of millionaires out there. There are a lot of young kids, and we can get a look at some who will really be good someday.'

The crowd that comes to see Lodigiani, between 2000 and 5000 each Saturday, is noticeably older than the normal *tifosi* who fill the Olimpico for Lazio or Roma. There are some talent scouts and others who are knowledgeable about the game, but mostly a large number of people who want to see a match in peace, and at a good price. 'You go to Stadio Olimpico and what do you get for it?' Calvani asks. 'It costs a bundle, you see the match badly, and it's dangerous. There's always some chance you're going to meet some *tifoso* from the other squad who's looking for trouble. People say it has calmed down, but that's not true. It may be calm at a place like Parma or Bologna, but at the big stadiums it's a mess.'

Flavio De Giovanni doesn't see it that way. The 24-year-old Roma supporter is one of about 10,000 who stand each Sunday in the *Curva Sud* of the Olimpico. He's been going to see Roma for five years, and paid 250,000 lire (£85) this season for seventeen home games. 'There may be some scuffles every once in a while, but basically it's pretty calm,' De Giovanni says. 'And at the big games, like the derby with Lazio, there are so many police that it's almost impossible for anything to happen.'

Italian police come out in force – helicopters, horses, the whole bit – for any match in which they suspect there might be trouble. In Rome and other big cities, rival supporters get a police escort to the other end of the stadium, away from the *curva* in which the ardent home supporters chant, sing, bang on drums and throw flares on to the field. The firemen in Rome have grown used to the flares, and they hose down the track surrounding the field before every game.

Despite all the police presence, frisking is somewhat haphazard. The flares get sneaked in, often with the organized groups, as they bring in their banners and drums and other accessories. 'At times they'll be real diligent frisking you,' De Giovanni said, 'but other times they're not very thorough at all.' So flares get in taped to the body, and lead pellets can be concealed in sandwiches. Two other favourite objects to throw, coins and lighters, are supposedly prohibited, but the security are more concerned about keeping rival supporters separated than they are about flying objects. If one Roma supporter in the lower *curva* gets hit by a flare or a lighter thrown from the upper *curva*, well, that's his problem. Italians may be mad about football, and there are thousands in every big city who talk of nothing else, but with very few exceptions they don't drink themselves into a stupor before, during or after a match. And that simple sociological fact does wonders for crowd control.

They still like fighting, throwing stones and bottles at police, and acting tough. But the last death that occurred from football violence, in January of 1995, shook the nation. Football matches and all other sporting events were cancelled the following Sunday after the stabbing to death of Genoa supporter Vincenzo Spagnolo. Genoa, then in Serie A, were playing at home against Milan, and Spagnolo got caught up in a pre-match rumble outside the ground. His killer, an 18-year-old *Milanista* named Simone Barbaglia, was quickly caught and found guilty of murder soon afterwards.

Barbaglia appeared to be truly repentant, and wrote a letter asking forgiveness of Spagnolo's parents. He was out of jail within a couple of years. 'The problem isn't the supporters,' said Enrico Spigone, an avid follower of Lazio. 'The problem is violence in general in society. Neither the kid who got killed nor the killer were deliquents. They were both decent guys.' Perhaps, but one did go to the stadium with a knife.

You don't see a lot of knives at the Tardini Stadium in Parma, not even in the *curva*, where the Boys make noise. You might see someone carrying a big plastic banana with the words 'Suck on This' scribbled on the side, but that's about the extent of Parma meanness. Vulgar but not violent. The *curva*'s favourite chorus is a sing-songy 'Go Bugger Yourself'; their bark is a lot worse than their bite. Even when a confused Napoli *tifoso* mistakenly wandered into the *curva* one day (wearing a Napoli shirt) he didn't suffer any bodily harm (which he might have in another stadium). Verbal abuse was enough to bring him to his senses, and make him look for another place to sit.

Paolo Melis, an engineering student, had season tickets to see Parma at home this year, and stood in the *Curva Nord*, although he was quick to point out that he wasn't one of the 'Boys', and doesn't like the word *ultra*. 'If Parma loses, I still sleep well,' Melis reported. The *curva* are the cheapest seats in the stadium, and Melis paid 315,000 lire (£110) for seventeen matches. Season tickets for good seats cost as much as £600, just as much as for the big teams and big stadiums.

The people of Parma frequently complain that the price of tickets is too high, while the team's directors complain that they don't get the kind of support they should from the city. 'Sometimes it sounds like there are more fans from the other team than from Parma,' Calisto Tanzi lamented. This is especially true for Parma–Juventus, given the overwhelming number of Juventus fans all around the country, including Parma.

While Melis and his friends watch the entire game standing – as happens in the *curva* of every stadium – the rich folks in the *tribuna* remain seated. 'They don't even stand up if we score a goal,' Melis said with a laugh. Parma had 19,000 season-ticket holders for 1997–98, and an average attendance of around 20,000. They reached near capacity, or 28,500, for Parma–Juventus. Visiting fans from the bigger squads, such as Milan, Lazio and Juve, could account for as many as 4000 fans.

Unlike Rome, Milan, or Florence, parents don't have to be worried about bringing their children to the stadium in Parma. Over the past five years, the number of 'incidents' involving *tifosi* can be counted on one hand. At Parma–Piacenza rock-throwing erupted outside the stadium, and a number of Roma fans got lost downtown once after a match and broke a few windows. Several years ago, a Parma fan was stabbed in the leg while in Turin for the Juventus match. But the incidents are all few and far between, and taking your family to see Parma is the equivalent of going to the cinema. A little more expensive, but not more dangerous or offensive. You hear a lot worse than 'Go Bugger Yourself' in most films.

While the only recent hooligan-related death came at the hands of a Milan supporter, the teams that traditionally have the most violent fans are Fiorentina, Atalanta of Bergamo and Brescia. Fiorentina sullied their violet shirts ten years ago when one of their roughnecks threw a Molotov cocktail into a train carriage bringing Bologna fans to Florence. While no one died, one Bologna fan – who still goes to Bologna matches – was badly disfigured. And because the action was pre-meditated, there was something more shocking about it than a fatal stabbing in a free-for-all brawl. More recently, the *Fiorentini* intercepted the bus carrying the Juventus squad outside the stadium and pelted it with rocks, breaking several windows.

Parma's February Italian Cup match with Atalanta was played on a neutral field rather than Bergamo because the Atalanta fans had rained coins upon the heads of the referee and linesmen in an earlier match that didn't finish in their favour. But coins are among the more innocent objects that have come down in Bergamo, where outraged *tifosi* have also been known to hurl screwdrivers on to the field.

Atalanta's *ultras* remain the closest Italy comes to English hooligans; they get just as much pleasure from doing battle with police as they do from fighting enemy fans. Perhaps more. Given that large numbers of the Atalanta fans come from the far political left, and frequent Bergamo's so-called 'social centres',★ there's no better enemy, no better institution for them to beat than the police. Bergamo's hooligans weren't happy about being relegated to Serie B, and disrupted the final game of the season against Juventus, tearing up the seats and throwing as much debris as possible on to the field. The match had to be suspended, and the club directors found themselves in the awkward position of trying to disassociate the team from its most ardent supporters.

★ The social centres for youth were meant to be cultural and educational alternatives to university back in the 1970s but they have evolved into state-funded recreational centres for the unemployed, usually with heavy political overtones.

★   ★   ★

Stefano Pietrangeli, 21, works in his family's coffee bar in downtown Rome. It's a good thing the bar's closed on Sunday, because every week when Lazio are in town, Pietrangeli is in the *curva nord* at Stadio Olimpico with his mom, dad, brother and girlfriend. They pay £100 a year each for season tickets. Lazio used to play at the smaller Stadio Flaminio, and Pietrangeli, who has been following the Eagles for ten years, preferred that smaller, warmer atmosphere to the enormous Olimpico. 'The Flaminio is marvellous, and you're so close that you can hear what the players are saying,' Pietrangeli said. 'It seems like you're on the field with them.'

Pietrangeli dislikes the organized fan groups such as the 'Eagle Supporters' and the '*Irriducibili*' since they become 'too politicized'. That means right. Although there are exceptions, and Rome's progressive mayor, Francesco Rutelli, is a *Laziale*, in general Lazio appeal to a conservative *tifoso*, while the *Romanisti* come from the poor neighbourhoods and vote leftist.★ It is no surprise that Massimo D'Alema, head of the Democratic Left, a modern version of the old Italian Communist Party, brings his young son to see Roma. The organized groups of *tifosi* have also gotten more negative, Pietrangeli claims, and no longer support their own squad as much as they attack the other one.

The match of the season for a *Laziale* is the derby with Roma. 'I start thinking about it two or three weeks before it's going to take place,' Pietrangeli explains. 'I talk with my friends who support Roma, and we make some bets. Then I buy all the sports papers, see all the television programmes about football, and listen to the radio. I don't want to miss a thing. What I hate is when the players are too diplomatic in the interviews. You'd think they were at a meeting of scientists, or something like that.'

Pietrangeli admits that he's not one who prays often, but normally makes an exception before the derby. 'When we get close

★ Not all of the working classes are *Romanisti*, however; the small towns outside of Rome are heavily *Laziale*.

to the big day I don't eat much, and on the Saturday night before, I'm so nervous that I normally don't sleep.' Pietrangeli goes to the game a couple hours ahead of time and waits with his friends. If Lazio lost the last game he attended, he doesn't stand in the same spot he did during that match. Pietrangeli defines the last half-hour before the game starts as 'the most beautiful part of the afternoon' because of the energy of the fans and the choruses.

Then the game starts, and like the rest of the *curva*, he remains standing. He sits only at half-time, in order to rest and read the fan paper.* Once, after the match, he tried getting one of the jerseys that the players throw into the crowd. 'But I've never seen such a fight,' he recalls. 'There was kicking, punching, people bleeding, and I've never tried again.' The matches start at 4 p.m. at the beginning and the end of the season, and 2:30 p.m. in the winter months. If Lazio wins, Pietrangeli races home on his scooter to watch all the football programmes on television, and stays up until past midnight. If they lose, he pretends nothing happened and doesn't even turn on the TV.

* A fan paper is a small newspaper given out for free at the stadium; it's frequently not very good, and is normally produced by one of the fan clubs. There are usually no programmes, only for the journalists (a kind of folder with all the relative stats inside).

8 Cheers and Tears: On Coaching in Italy

After the first game of the season, Fiorentina coach Alberto Malesani was in tears, jumping up and down like a kid in front of the *curva* where the hard-core supporters watch the game. The Mister was dressed in shorts and at 43, Malesani was one of the youngest coaches in the league. Only Ancelotti and Luciano Spalletti of Empoli were younger. Malesani not only looks young, he acts young, and isn't afraid to show his emotions. But Malesani had every right to cry. His debut in Serie A came off successfully: a 2−1 come-from-behind victory away over Udinese.

'I probably had accumulated so much tension thinking about how important it was to win,' Malesani recalls. 'Before the season began I was already being criticized by some fans. Then we were losing 1−0 up until five minutes before the end of the game. So showing my emotions was kind of a release of all that tension.'

The joys of coaching can be intense. Ancelotti remembers particularly bringing Reggiana, after that horrendous start, into Serie A. But the disappointments, pain and outright sorrows tend to outweigh the glory. Ten games after his tears of joy, Malesani would have to face his intrusive owner, Vittorio Cecchi Gori, in the dressing room − in the middle of the match − yelling and telling him who he should put in the game.

Malesani insists that he wasn't humiliated. 'Maybe the time and the place were wrong, but you're the employee; you better listen to the guy who pays you,' the Mister said. But that didn't make life for Malesani any easier, and by the beginning of April he had still not renewed his contract, despite the Mister being popular with both players and fans. For a first-year coach, Malesani was having a good season, and Fiorentina had excellent chances of finishing in the top six, thereby qualifying for the UEFA Cup. But Cecchi Gori insisted that he'd make a decison at the end of the season.

This was, of course, similar to Ancelotti's situation at Parma. There were newspaper reports (rumours, really) at the end of February that Parma had already contacted Malesani about coming to them the following season. And without a vote of confidence from his owner, the young coach would have every reason to try somewhere else, especially a squad with money to spend. Malesani said he wanted to stay at Fiorentina, but that the choice wasn't his.

Football friendships between owners and coaches are short-lived in Italy, and loyalty lasts only as long as you win. Only a few Italian Serie A misters in the post-war period have remained with the same team for, say, ten years in a row. The best example is Giovanni Trapattoni, who guided Juventus from 1976 to 1986. There were good reasons for his longevity. 'Trap' won six *scudetti* in ten seasons. Nevio Scala, now at Borussia Dortmund, could have matched that. He spent seven seasons at Parma (one in Serie B and six in A), but there was a sense that a certain cycle had ended, and it was time to move on.

The new cycle started with Ancelotti, and got off to a great start. At the end of his first season, after they had clinched 2nd place and a berth in the Champions League, Ancelotti celebrated with club president Stefano Tanzi and his sister Francesca, a member of the board of Parma Calcio. A smiling Enrico Chiesa stripped down to his underwear to celebrate with the Boys and defender Fabio Cannavaro ambushed Stefano Tanzi, showering him with champagne. Those were the good times, and the proof that Ancelotti could make it in the big league. But less than twelve months later his stock had dropped and the brother and sister were already sniffing around for a new manager.

Bologna's outspoken coach, Renzo Ulivieri, claims he lives in constant fear of his team being sent down to Serie B, clearly the best way for a Serie A coach to lose his job. 'We've all got this fear, and let me tell you that on Sunday it's particularly bad,' Ulivieri says. 'Take the fear of San Siro, for example. It's wonderful. I highly recommend it. And the great thing is that it disappears when you discover that even at San Siro they play football with a ball and two goals. And you might even manage to score a goal more than the other guys.'

Ulivieri was well liked by Bologna fans – a left-winger who enjoys talking politics, he was well-suited to Bologna, a notoriously 'red' city – and when it became clear that he would be sacked after four seasons with the squad, graffiti appeared near the training ground imploring the owners to keep him. 'Renzo For Ever,' the *tifosi* wrote. But it was no use. Ulivieri was gone, and down to Serie B. He had chosen to go with Naples, who were having a terrible season. And why does a well-respected and well-liked Serie A coach voluntarily step down into B? 'My decisions have never been particularly rational,' Ulivieri said. 'Naples were the first people to give me an offer.' Bologna, after Malesani refused them, later tried to get Ulivieri to stay, but this time it was his turn tell them to get lost.

Ulivieri said his Sunday morning jitters are exactly like those of taking a test. Once it starts, the nervousness disappears. But after it's over, it can start up again. 'On Sunday nights I'm agitated,' Ulivieri said. 'If I won, I watch TV – all the sports shows – until three in the morning. If I lost, I still watch TV, but it's not the same.' Ulivieri called coaching 'as fascinating as it is difficult' and figured that his hardest task each week was not making a plan to stop the other team's attack but telling six players that they would have to watch the game on Sunday from the stands. Ulivieri said you have to put the pressure – from owners, fans and the press – in perspective. 'I don't have problems,' he stated, flatly. 'Sometimes they have problems with me.'

Luciano Spalletti of Empoli was a victim of his own success. Spalletti brought Empoli up from B in the 1996–97 season, and suddenly found himself at the head of a squad that was going to have to face the giants called Inter, Juventus and Milan. 'As a player I was never great, and for me Serie A was always a kind of dream, something sacred,' he explains. 'Now that I'm in this dream I'm afraid of waking up. I think it's a legitimate feeling.'

Call it fear, call it stress, call it pressure. The fans, the press and the owners all expect victories. The weight falls on the players, but above all on the coach. 'If the team wins, the players get the credit, but if they lose it's the coach's fault,' notes Ancelotti.

Malesani, well tanned with shaggy hair and sharp sunglasses, looks more like a laid-back ski instructor than the Mister on one of the most volatile teams in Serie A. 'You know from the start that there are going to be some confrontations,' he says. 'The press, for example, can give you problems. But you need the equilibrium to handle those things.' Fiorentina also have a lively and vociferous group of fans (about 1000 come every day just to watch training), a wildman for an owner, and several big-ego, big-paycheque players. 'Whenever I have problems I always think of how many colleagues I have who would like to be coaching one of the eighteen teams in Serie A,' Malesani says, with a laugh.

While Ancelotti and his players can walk around Parma practically undisturbed, Malesani and his charges can hardly move in Florence without being touched, talked to, and besieged for autographs. 'Yeah,' admits the Mister. 'Here they treat you like you're important.' And the coach is important; his decisions will make the difference between victory and defeat.

That excessive attention adds up to quite a bit of stress on Sunday. 'I feel the most tension in the few hours right before the game,' says Malesani. 'I speak to the players in the morning and for two hours leave them alone. During that time I try to just stay focused on our tactics. Then once the ref blows the whistle for the start of the game, all the tension disappears. But that doesn't mean it's not going to come back afterwards.'

Malesani quickly admits that he was never a great player. He made it to Serie C as a midfielder, but his career was short-lived. Before he became a full-time coach, he worked for twelve years in Verona in the import/export divison of Canon Italia, the camera makers. 'I used to continually struggle to get a raise,' he recalled. 'Now the figures are a little different, but they're two different worlds.'

Two different worlds, yes. But Malesani believes the business experience he had was useful for coaching. 'It's been helpful in terms of programming and planning,' he noted. Part of that planning was knowing how to say no the first time he got an offer to coach in Serie A. He waited until he was ready and had the chance to go with a competitive team. That still didn't mean he'd have a job after one season, but he had managed to prove himself as a capable coach.

But, ultimately, that wasn't enough. Managers come and go at the owner's latest whim. Fiorentina picked up Alberto Malesani, one of the few Italian coaches currently favouring the offensive and exciting 3–4–3 (Zaccheroni of Udinese is another, along with Zeman at Roma as well) and then sacked him after only a year, to begin negotiations with Giovanni Trapattoni, 59, whose style is essentially the opposite. Trapattoni has been managing since 1973 and plays an extremely conservative game, basically the conservative old Italian *catenaccio*, or big dirty chain.

Out with Malesani after only a year and in with Trapattoni. It was a textbook example of fickle football ownership. Long-range planning has never been the forte of wealthy Italians. As Vaccari said: 'If you don't know where you're going it's difficult to get there,' adding that Naples and Inter and the other squads in A were not much different from Fiorentina in this regard. 'This isn't a country in which you manage to do much medium or long-range planning. It's all for the next day.'

Coaching in Italy is similar to driving; you don't do it without a licence. But it's a little harder to get that piece of paper, especially if you want to be in the driver's seat of one of eighteen teams in Serie A or twenty in Serie B. Malesani complains that he spent all his vacation time in the classroom at Coverciano, the football federation's school for coaches in Florence. There are two courses for professional coaches: 'Second Category' for those in C1 and

C2, and the 'Master' for those in Serie A and B. But before that you have to have a 'Basic' degree in coaching.

Selection at Coverciano is tough. 'You'd never get in,' Ancelotti told me, as he talked about his experience there, and he's right. It's like getting accepted at Harvard Business School. Some forty are taken each summer for the Second Category, but only twenty for the Master. And before they'll even look at a candidate, he has to have his Basic title. Then it depends on what his record as a coach has been, and if he has any experience as a player.

'There are no set rules about players and coaches,' says Gianni Leali, 52, head of the school. 'You can't say a good player doesn't make a good coach, or that if someone didn't play well he won't know how to run a team. Malesani was never a great player but he has proven to be a good mister.' Most of the coaches in Serie A were run-of-the-mill players. Ancelotti's career was an exception, far ahead of the average.

Some 40,000 Italians have been licensed as Basic coaches, allowing them to train amateur teams. 'In Italy, everyone wants to be a coach,' says Leali, who has written several books on coaching and formerly taught 'training theory'. Foreigners can coach in Italy, but they have to have an accredited Italian by their side on the bench. Such is the case with Eriksson, at Lazio, who is teamed up with Luciano Spinosi.

Leali believes Italian football underwent a transformation in the 1970s, after the success of the dynamic Dutch teams led by Johann Cruyff. 'Before that it was football *all'italiana*,' he says, 'with the stopper, a solid defence and the counter-attack.' That was the basis of the 1960s Inter, a team famous for its *catenaccio*.★ 'Holland's success was instrumental in making Italian coaches a little more

★ *Catenaccio* means the team parks itself in its own half of the pitch, perhaps with only one striker out towards midfield. They wait for the other side to take the initiative and don't press. It's essentially what most teams are forced to do when they're down a man, hoping that they manage to score on the counter-attack. Italian teams used to play this way all the time.

open-minded,' Leali notes. 'A lot of teams got rid of the stopper and added the *terzini* [lateral full-backs] who could also attack.'

Some Italian teams play with four backs; others with three. On attack, they also vary between two and three. The classical formation today (like Parma's) is the 4–4–2, but others play with a 3–4–3 or a 3–5–2. 'There's a variety, and that makes the championship a lot more interesting,' Leali said. For instance, in defence, the squads play man-to-man, zonal, or a mixed system. Ancelotti, a faithful disciple of Sacchi, sticks strictly to the zonal defence, while Marcello Lippi of Juventus has his backs play man-to-man and his midfield play zonal. 'We don't teach one system,' Leali continues. 'We teach them all, and then show the advantages and disadvantages of each one.'

Variety abounds in Serie A. Roma play an explosive and fast attack-oriented game; Inter show much more prudence with their solid defence and midfield, relying on the counter-attack for many of their goals. But it's not the various styles of play that make Serie A so interesting; it's the abundance of talent. 'Our championship is the most difficult in the world,' Leali said. 'That's not an opinion but a fact. In Holland you've got two teams that are above all the rest. Here there's a lot more equilibrium among the squads. And this season's a good example. It's uncertain at the top – who will win the *scudetto* – and uncertain at the bottom; who will be relegated.'

Ronaldo's Spanish experience offers a good comparison. In 37 games in La Liga, Ronaldo scored 34 goals. But in 34 Serie A matches, he managed 'only' 25, and six of those were penalty shots. Anyone else would have been happy with those 25 goals, which were a record for a foreigner playing for the first time in Italy, but Ronaldo's diminished performance reflected not so much anything that had happened to him, but the strength of Italian football. 'Strikers often score because of their ability, but also because of defensive errors,' Leali said. 'And in Italy our defenders are traditionally very strong. Fewer errors means fewer goals.'

Ancelotti received the highest mark possible (110 *e Lode* – A+) on his thesis, entitled *Offensive Movements in a 4–4–2 System of*

Play. They could have hardly given him a lower grade. The Mister had just finished his first year as a coach by leading his team to 2nd place in Serie A. What were they going to do, flunk him?*

The student-Mister wrote nine chapters in the fifty-two-page thesis, ranging from 'The Pass' and 'Ball Possession' to 'Psychological Aspects in Teaching'. There are also more than twenty diagrams that explain movements on the field.

Ancelotti clearly wrote from experience, not from anything he learned in books or in the classroom. 'In the last few years in Italy, we've paid a lot of attention to defensive tactics,' he said in his introduction. 'A lot of managers have spent the greater part of their time in finding effective solutions to block or interrupt the offensive capabilities of their adversaries. The need for clubs to have positive results right away, and the fear of managers of getting fired, has accentuated this aspect of the game. It's difficult to find teams, whether they play man-to-man or zone, who don't have a good defensive organization.'

Despite the need for solid defence, Ancelotti noted that the public is looking for a product that's more 'spectacular' and that the future is likely to bring football that's more dynamic on account of the rhythm with which it's played, and the variety of attacks. 'It's fundamental to have a tactical plan in which the eleven players move in a synchronized fashion, and that it be the fruit of the individual and collective culture of the player,' he wrote. 'If in making a film, there's a script to be followed . . . even in football there will also be a kind of script, and a player will be better inasmuch as he manages to interpret it, enriching it with his own variations.'

That analogy was about as deep as the Mister got in his thesis. Much of the rest was good, common football sense, with a few interesting facts thrown in for good measure. For example:

* While at Reggiana Ancelotti was technically 'illegal' since he didn't have the licence yet, and after his first season in Serie A at Parma he still had to get his Masters.

* 'To make the play effective it's absolutely necessary that movement without the ball and the pass be perfectly synchronized.'
* 'It's been proven that during the 90 minutes of a game, each player has possession of the ball for somewhere between 4 seconds and 3 minutes and 30 seconds.'
* 'Movement of the ball becomes sterile if it's not accompanied by the right movement of the player.'
* 'The more the players manage to move in a synchronized manner, the more our attack will be varied, effective, unforseeable, and imaginative.'
* 'If the midfielder who's about to receive the ball is marked, the movement of the other midfielder will be in support of his companion who's in trouble.'
* 'One has to be careful with possession. It's certainly effective if it's aimed at constructing an attack, but can be deleterious if it's used in a static and passive way.'

The thesis also includes several training drills, illustrated with diagrams. Ancelotti also wrote about 'verticalization', a word that's used frequently in Italian football commentary to describe bringing the ball upfield. 'It doesn't [just] mean long balls, since in every circumstance it's better to have a precise pass ahead that gains ground,' Ancelotti said.

Clear enough. Ancelotti concluded as he began, talking about how Italian football has become too defensive, since the clubs want to 'win at all costs' while the fans are, at the same time, looking for more excitement. 'We have to turn our attention to the collective movements of the team, and the quickness of thought of each athlete,' he wrote. 'If some years ago one of the qualities that distinguished a star was his technical skill, now the great player also stands out because of his capacity to foresee or anticipate his own play or that of an opponent.'

While Ancelotti talked about attack, and the need to give the fans something 'spectacular', the lack of attack would get him in trouble at Parma. Even when they finished 2nd in the 1996–97 season, it wasn't because they were blowing the other teams away with scores of 3–0 or 4–1. As Calisto Tanzi described it, Parma would score a goal 'and then make the fans suffer for the rest of the game'. The owner mused that maybe it was better to win 5–3.

9 The Tower of Babel

Walter Veltroni, Deputy Prime Minister and the would-be Tony Blair of Italian politics, also serves as Minister of Culture and delegate for sport. Former editor of the official daily of the Democratic Party of the Left, *L'Unita*, Veltroni has good credentials as a progressive thinker. Not a hard-core leftist, but a kind of radical chic, Bobby Kennedy figure. He's also a passionate Juventus fan.

But when it comes to football, Veltroni wants no team to be able to field more than five non-Italians at a time. This is good old-fashioned Italian protectionism at work, the kind of stuff that has kept auto giant Fiat profitable. Veltroni wants to give Serie A back to the Italians. In the aftermath of the Bosman ruling, the championship has become a kind of Tower of Babel. The eighteen teams in Serie A this year had 117 non-Italians on their rosters, up from 98 the previous season, and 66 during the '95–96 season.

The guilty parties? If they weren't already sponsored by Pirelli, Inter might as well be wearing the United Nations logo on their jerseys. When the players' market closed in January '98, they had 13 foreigners; 8 from the EC, 3 Latin Americans and 2 Africans. Milan had 12 foreigners and Roma 11. But of these only Inter were in the running for the *scudetto*. In Serie A Piacenza had the lone distinction of fielding an all-Italian squad. And it showed. They struggled to stay in the division, eventually finishing 13th.

But that didn't mean that *stranieri* (literally 'strangers'), high-priced Brazilians and Frenchmen, guaranteed victories, as AC Milan owner Silvio Berlusconi discovered to his great surprise. The best players at Milan all featured in their respective national squads – France, Brazil, Germany, Italy and Holland – yet manager Fabio Capello still couldn't find the right combination for Serie

96

A. Milan spent the first half of the season below mid-table, and struggled all season just to get near the UEFA zone.

Walter Veltroni wants to find the equilibrium between EC regulations (free circulation of EC residents) and what he calls the 'development of the football tradition of each country'. In other words, he's worried that the very success of Serie A, which is based largely on the presence of the boys from Brazil and their buddies from Argentina, is damaging Italian football. If Inter has 48,000 season-ticket holders, that's in large part due to a 22-year-old called the Phenomenon. But Ronaldo's presence on the pitch also means there's probably some young, able-bodied Italian striker who's not going to have the chance to show his stuff.

Veltroni's proposal, which he has brought to the EC, is relatively simple: no limit to the number of foreigners on the roster; no distinction between EC and non-EC citizens; but a team can put only five foreigners on the field at a time. The second point, about EC and non-EC citizens, makes perfect sense. Regulations currently allow for an unlimited number of non-Italians, but no more than three from outside the EC on the pitch or on the bench at one time.

Veltroni's levelling the field on that count would help do away with some of the contortions that currently take place, such as the effort to make any Argentinian with an Italian name a citizen, or searching for the great-great-great-great-great-grandparents of a star striker just in case they might have visited Italy once; the old honeymoon = citizenship trick. It's not quite that bad, but pretty close. Roma's Brazilian defender Aldair and Argentinian forward Albo Balbo are both certified Italians, as are two Argentinians on Lazio, Josh Chamot and Matias Almeyda.

Veltroni's idea of moderate protectionism has been greeted positively, at least on first glance, by fourteen of the eighteen squads in Serie A. Parma were willing to accept a limit, but stressed that it had to be implemented gradually over a period of several years, and not from one season to the next. The *gialloblu* occasionally run into trouble because they have four non-ECers (Hernán Crespo of Argentina, Zé Maria and Bolzan Adailton of Brazil, and Mario

Stanic of Croatia) and Ancelotti is forced to keep one of them out every game. Fortunately midfielder Nestor Sensini is an Argentine-Italian.

As far as the fans are concerned, the question of foreigners in the Italian game is one that leads to spirited debate. While foreign players have raised the level of the game, and make every Sunday showtime, there are those who argue that too many foreigners are detrimental to the prospects of the national team. And, of course, foreigners don't always flourish in Italian football, which is defence-minded, and sometimes obsessively so. No other country is renowned for its *catenaccio*. Dennis Bergkamp, for instance, never made it big at Inter, scoring only 11 goals in two seasons, even though he was there at that same time as his Dutch buddy Wim Jonk. Bergkamp says he left because he couldn't manage to play his game when the whole idea was defence. 'I'm a striker who's got to be on a team that's always looking to score,' Bergkamp says. He was in the wrong country. And yet he notes that Serie A is practically an obligatory stop for someone who wants to show his skills to the world.

The football trinity that turned Milan into a mini-dynasty in the 1990s was Dutch, made up of Ruud Gullit, Frank Rikaard and Marco Van Basten, but after that the Netherlands hasn't managed to send such a talented batch of players to Serie A. Bergkamp and Jonk tried at Inter; Patrick Kluivert and Winston Bogarde have been big disappointments for Milan. The Swedes have been playing better in Italy than the Dutch, especially Kennet Andersson at Bologna, Jesper Blomqvist at Parma and Stefan Schwarz at Florence.

The English have practically disappeared from Italian football. David Platt played in a weak Bari squad in 1991–92, got sold to Juve when Bari were relegated, but didn't get to play enough because Juventus was too strong. From there he went to Sampdoria of Genova, where he got to play more but still couldn't shine. Paul Gascoigne performed (and performed is the right word) erratically at Lazio and Paul Ince played well, if not spectacularly, at Roy Hodgson's Inter before returning home after a year, leaving no Englishmen in Serie A. It's been a long time, forty years to be exact, since John Charles played at Juventus.

As for English football, most Italians will argue that it's still quite a bit inferior to the Italian game, especially in terms of tactics. It's viewed mainly as a 'kick and run' game, and there is also the suspicion that the training is not as intense. 'Why do you think Di Matteo isn't a starter any more on the national team?' asks Filippo Ferrari, a political science student from Bergamo. 'He's clearly fallen out of form.'

Spaniards are also missing in Serie A. Martín Vazquez came from Real Madrid and played solid football at Torino in the early nineties, but the teams in La Liga now have enough money to keep their own boys at home, as Parma learned when they were chasing Barcelona's Josep Guardiola. Foreigners who fit in well in Italy are the Argentinians (many of them are of Italian descent anyway, can get Italian passports easily and quickly learn the language), French and Brazilians. Except, of course, for the Animal, Edmundo.

Italian national team coach Cesare Maldini laments the fact there are so many foreigners in Serie A. They take away playing time for his own boys, and keep young Italians from showing their potential. 'Over the last few years I see that the major Italian clubs, the ones up for Cup titles, have motors – and the motor for me is the midfield – that are foreign legions,' Maldini said. 'They're all foreigners. The only major Italian team with an all-Italian midfield is Roma. All the rest have a minimum of two foreigners. In that sense our players don't have a chance to improve.'

The 'foreign' question would return after the all-Italian UEFA Cup Final, between Inter and Lazio. It wasn't really 'all-Italian', given the make-up of Inter. They celebrated a Latin American night in Paris, as a Chilean, an Argentine and a Brazilian (or more precisely, *the* Brazilian) scored for Inter in their 3–0 victory. Ivan Zamorano put Inter on top just four minutes into the game; Javier Zanetti extinguished any hope Lazio still harboured at the start of the second half, and Ronaldo added one for the record books before it was over.

Inter's victory in the UEFA Cup came as a kind of consolation after having failed to win the *scudetto*, but not everyone was rejoicing with them. 'I can't manage to get excited about a team that has almost nothing left that's Italian on it,' said Mario Pescante, head of the Italian Olympic Committee, and one of the most important sports figures in the country. Indeed, Inter started only three Italians in the game and had two sitting on the bench. The rest was a mix of France, Holland, Latin America and Africa.

'So why isn't Chelsea an Italian team?' asked Lanfranco Vaccari, deputy editor of *La Gazzetta dello Sport*. 'Just like Inter, they send three Italians on to the field and they have an Italian coach.' The Bosman decision has led to a watering down of the national character of the squads, and Vaccari sees it as a negative development. 'There are no longer players who are identified with the squad,' he said, accusing the players of being 'mercenaries without principles and even less loyalty, attracted only by money, and ready to be a traitor if someone offers more.'

Vaccari charged that the new, multi-nation teams were capable of playing great football, but that the squads had lost their souls. Inter's president Massimo Moratti, who was carried on the shoulders of his boys after the UEFA victory, didn't want to hear about Internazionale having lost its *italianita*. 'These are old stories,' Moratti said. 'The players are good and that's that.' Not everyone agreed. Parma supporter Andrea Pelosio recalled doing the count on Inter for an early UEFA Cup match and coming up with only two Italians among the starters. 'If I were an *Interista* I'd be embarrassed,' he said.

Among managers, Italians have had extraordinary success abroad. Fabio Capello went to Real Madrid and won the Spanish championship in 1997, despite the formidable presence of Ronaldo at rival Barcelona, where he scored nearly a goal a game. In Germany during the same year, Giovanni Trapattoni, formerly with Juve and Inter, won the Bundesliga with Bayern Munich, while in Switzerland Italian manager Albertino Bigon won both the league championship and the Swiss Cup at Sion. Coaching is serious business for Italians.

Trapattoni later got into trouble at Bayern when he blasted his players for being unprofessional and lazy – his outcry, in stilted German, was later put to music, as the 'Trap Rap' – but his record as a manager remains outstanding. 'Italians, by a long shot, make the best misters in the world,' claims Giorgio Tosatti, one of the top football commentators in Italy. 'In a lot of countries, there's one kind of football, and everybody plays it. Here there are a lot of different versions of the game, and every coach has his own concept. So it's a lot more complicated. Italy is the university of world football, and to teach here you really have to be good.'

In Italy, though, most foreigners, and especially Latin Americans, have struggled in management. Tosatti notes that most of the foreigners who have coached in Italy have been out after a year, although he quickly adds that he believes Roy Hodgson, who made an early exit from Inter, to be a good coach. Latin Americans have been especially quick to get the boot. Oscar Washington Tabarez of Uruguay lasted just 11 games with Milan in 1996, and Luis Cesar Menotti of Argentina was out of Sampdoria only ten weeks into the season in 1997. Fellow Argentine Carlos Bianchi had lasted a little longer with Roma during the 1996–97 season: 26 games.

No foreign manager has become a legend at an Italian team since Spaniard Helenio Herrera ran Inter in the 1960s, when Moratti's father owned the team. Nils Liedholm of Sweden distinguished himself at Milan with a *scudetto* in 1979, and made his mark with Roma in the 1980s with a *scudetto* and three Italian Cups. Another Swede, Sven Goran Eriksson, may have a chance with Lazio. Eriksson won the championship in Portugal three times at Benfica, but in his ten years in Serie A before coming to Lazio the best he did was a 2nd-place finish at Roma in 1986 and 3rd place for Sampdoria in 1994. Zeman, currently at Roma, has the right stuff to win a *campionato*, but probably needs a different squad.

Tosatti believes Italian players are tactically much better prepared than those in other countries, and more aware of possible failings on the part of the coach. 'They don't put up with stupid professors,' he says, bluntly. And Tosatti says that the coaching school at Coverciano, just outside of Florence, is not simply a bureaucratic hurdle, but provides serious training. 'We don't turn players into coaches overnight,' he snorts, referring to Gianluca Vialli's promotion to player-coach at Chelsea after player-coach Ruud Gullit got the boot. 'Those are childhood games.'

At the end of the season, Lazio would be busy in the players' market, working to sell Vladimir Jugovic to Atlético Madrid, Pierluigi Casiraghi to Chelsea, and Diego Fuser to Parma, among other deals. But owner Sergio Cragnotti's biggest surprise was signing an Argentinian, Julio Velasco, as general director. Although he had also been courted by other clubs, including Milan, Velasco made a name for himself in volleyball, and was manager of the Italian national team for nine years, in which they won everything but the Olympics. *Corriere dello Sport*, in typically exaggerated tones, described him as 'a man who was born to succeed'. Lazio weren't the first Italian club to bring in a director who hadn't grown up working in football. Three years earlier Parma had found new blood in the volleyball business, and hired away two youngsters, Michele Uva as executive director and Giorgio Bottaro as team spokesman.

10 March

Bologna v Parma
March 1 1998

Renzo Ulivieri must really not like Ancelotti very much. Bologna's coach had only managed to beat Carlo's squads once in the seven times they'd met, and the return leg of this season offered more of the same. Ulivieri was prohibited from sitting on the bench after picking up a two-game disqualification for having argued too much during a Roma–Bologna match. So he was up at the top of the stands, near the television cameras, brooding as his boys took an early lead, lost it four minutes later, and lost the game 15 minutes after that. It finished 2–1 – an away victory for Ancelotti providing three points, and what he hoped would be the turn-around for the rest of the season.

It was also a beautiful game, one of those rare Serie A events in which both teams actually want to win. A sunny Sunday afternoon and a packed stadium made it even more of an attraction. It was also the closest match Parma had to a derby, since Bologna sits just 85 kilometres south-east from the home of the *gialloblu*. Bologna's glory years are gone – they have won seven *scudetti*, five of which are from the 1920s and 30s – but they still field a respectable team, which includes playmaker Roberto Baggio, the tall Swedish forward Kennet Andersson, and the dangerous Russian Igor Kolyvanov. Missing against Parma was Stefano Torrisi, a midfielder who was suspended.

Ancelotti had almost his entire squad, although he was missing injured defender Antonio Benarrivo and midfielder Nestor Sensini. The Mister put Crespo on the bench, starting Mario Stanic in atttack with Enrico Chiesa. Crespo had just returned from Argentina, where he scored a hat-trick for the national team. Why he never managed to score three for Parma was one of those riddles Ancelotti was trying to solve. But in the meantime, Stanic, normally a midfielder, had scored two goals in two games since being moved up to the front line. Taking advantage of an error by the Bologna keeper, Stanic headed in the equalizer for Parma just four minutes after Bologna had scored from a corner kick.

Although Bologna dominated the first 15 minutes of the game, Parma were not playing badly, and there were opportunities to score on both sides of the field. But Gigi Buffon was outstanding in goal, making three great saves, and two extraordinary ones. The 20-year-old keeper dominated the headlines the following day, as the papers shouted BUFFON MAKES THE DIFFERENCE and BUF-FON HYPNOTIZES BOLOGNA. The game could have finished 2–2 or 3–3 and no one would have felt cheated. Or it might have ended up 4–1 for Bologna, had Buffon not robbed Baggio, Koly-vanov and Andersson of goals.

Buffon showed his great instincts, but was also aided by a little luck. Four minutes into injury time, as Parma players prayed for the final whistle to blow, Carlo Nervo lobbed a cross over the young keeper that hit the crossbar. Bologna fans thought they had been robbed of penalty kicks on two occasions (one was a very clear but involuntary hand by Dino Baggio) and heaped abuse upon the referee, Cosimo Bolognino.

Ancelotti was ecstatic and stayed on the pitch for several minutes, walking over to the corner reserved for visiting fans and waving his hat to the Parma faithful. As he walked the length of the field he also greeted the brass from Parma sitting in the good seats, a section known as the *Honor Tribune*. But the Parma supporters were far outnumbered by Bologna fans, who despite paying top dollar for their seats, still greeted his wave with enthusiastic suggestions that he go bugger himself.

Bologna was Buffon's great day, and certainly earned him some points on the national team. But he still saw himself far from the starting role, currently held by Juve's keeper, Angelo Peruzzi. 'I've got to play about thirty games like the one on Sunday,' said Buffon, happy that he got applause even from Bologna fans for a few of his saves. *Corriere dello Sport* gave him a 9 for the game, claiming he was the keeper everyone would want for their own team, a 'phenomenon for his sense of position, ability to explode and maturity'.

But the Bologna game also signalled a certain sense of maturity in the entire Parma squad, who for the second week in a row managed to come from behind and win a game. 'We had the right reaction,' Ancelotti said. 'We didn't get demoralized and we played well.' At least for a while. Parma suffered Bologna's attacks in the second half even after Bologna captain Giancarlo Marocchi was sent off for contesting too many of the referee's decisions. The Mister worried that Parma would not hold on to the lead, and was especially impressed with Roberto Baggio and Andersson, whom he defined as 'practically unmarkable on headers'.

Roberto Baggio, who worked his first miracles in his early twenties at Fiorentina, and then went on to become one of the country's favourites at Juventus, has reached that age in which most offensive players begin to wane. Baggio, 31, is no exception. And yet he still has flashes of brilliance – he played extremely well against Parma – and was chasing a place on the national team that was going to France for the World Cup.

Baggio lost some of his hair this season, and was playing without his trademark ponytail, but had retained many of his old moves. 'He's in good shape and he created a lot of difficulties for us,' Ancelotti said. 'If he continues like this he can certainly aspire to a spot on the national team.'

Baggio would have scored the equalizer with a header aimed for the lower left-hand corner had it not been for Buffon's prodigious dive. But in the first half he also ate an easy goal and let the keeper smother a ball he should have put in the net.

The fact is that Baggio is no longer the *trascinatore* that some fans believe him to be. There was a campaign to get him to the World Cup – in the end, a successful one – but the facts spoke for themselves. After 23 games he had 13 goals. Not bad at all, but 7 were penalties. None of those who were plugging Roby so enthusiastically seemed to rememer that Baggio's most famous penalty shot, in the final game of the 1994 World Cup in Los Angeles, went flying over the crossbar, and he walked off the pitch in tears. Baggio was on a mission this season, and wanted only a chance to redeem himself. Maldini called him up to play against Poland, and Roby scored a goal. He took one step closer to Paris, and at this point in his career, the World Cup – just one more chance – was all that mattered.

Baggio is probably the best-known Italian player worldwide, and Japanese fans make pilgrimages to Bologna just to get a glimpse at him during training. But he's also somebody who sat on the bench for most of his time at Milan and would have spent a fair amount of time warming the wood at Parma as well. He stormed out of Bologna after Ulivieri kept him out of a game against Milan and told him he wouldn't be starting against Juventus. The Mister then threatened to resign when the owners didn't back him up. But the feisty manager finally came to terms with his owners, and Baggio regained his place as a starter.

Parma v Inter
March 8 1998

After his outstanding performance at Bologna, Gigi Buffon's mild self-criticism was that he had to become more consistent. He got off to a pretty good start with that resolution the following week when Parma kept Inter from scoring, and Hernán Crespo infiltrated the Inter defence on a corner kick to slam one in 30 minutes into the second half. It finished 1–0. Parma had knocked Inter out of 2nd place.

It can't be overstated: if Italians frequently play boring, defence-minded football, there's a reason for it. The team that concedes the fewest goals usually wins.* The top of the table by early March offered few exceptions to that rule. Juventus had given up 20 goals, Lazio 17, Inter 21 and Parma 23. The only mid-table team that had given up fewer goals than Parma was Milan, which had conceded 22.

With 10 games to go in the regular season, Juve held first place with 52 points, and were followed by Lazio (48), Inter (47) and Parma (44). Udinese were on Parma's heels with 43 points, and Roma were in 6th place with 41. Lazio's coach Sven Goran Eriksson refused to pronounce the word *scudetto* out of superstition, but it was pretty clear that the team was in the running for the title. Parma could still shoot for a Champions League berth.

Parma had, after all, stopped Inter, the team that spent the entire first half of the season at the top of the table. No, they did better than that. They beat Inter and, in particular, they beat Ronaldo. Or Buffon beat Ronaldo. The Phenomenon was awarded a rather dubious penalty 22 minutes into the second half. He takes nearly all Inter's free-kicks and penalties, and the game suddenly looked like it was going to end the same way the first leg did – 1–0 Inter, with a goal from Ronaldo. In November it was a free-kick just outside the area. This time it would be even easier.

The tension was high as Ronaldo prepared his shot. While most of the crowd were whistling at the Brazilian, there were a good number of *Interisti* at Tardini that afternoon, and they immediately sensed victory once the ref blew and Ronnie lined up for the shot.

Brazilian defender Zé Maria, who was called for the foul on Ronaldo, tried working his version of voodoo – something they call 'macumba' in Brazil – by touching the ball before Ronaldo kicked it and then telling Buffon which way he should dive. 'He knows Ronaldo a lot better than I do, but at that point you don't

---

* In the last ten years there have been only four occasions in which the championship-winning team didn't concede the least number of goals. One was this season, as Inter finished with 27 goals scored against them compared to Juve's 28. In 1994–95, Juve won the *scudetto* with 59 goals scored and 32 conceded, while 3rd-place Parma scored 51 and let in 31.

listen to anybody else,' Buffon said. 'You just follow your instincts.'

It came down to a game between boys: 21-year-old Ronaldo against 20-year-old Gigi Buffon. Buffon won, diving to his left and blocking the shot. The Phenomenon was stunned, left there scratching his close-shaved head. In the scuffle that followed on the rebound, there may have been a foul of Thuram on Inter's Diego Simeone, but the referee wasn't about to call a second penalty when he may have made a mistake on the first. Parma brought the ball downfield and Buffon celebrated with Parma's die-hard fans, the Boys, behind the goal.

People started calling Buffon 'Superman' after the match. Underneath his jersey he was wearing a Superman t-shirt that a woman from Naples had sent him. While the players in Serie A are extremely superstitious, Buffon insisted that the shirt wasn't a good-luck charm. 'I like the colours,' he said.

Buffon's instincts have proven to be pretty good, and in addition to Ronaldo he also stopped Youri Djorkaeff from short range. But Bologna had been an even a bigger test for him the previous week, since they kept him busier. At the end of 90 minutes, Inter had managed only three shots on goal, plus the penalty.

But whether he likes it or not (and he says he doesn't) Ronaldo is the Phenomenon and not everyone can stop him. 'Sure, he made something of a mistake, but I didn't give him any help,' Buffon said. 'I waited until the last possible minute.' Parma owner Calisto Tanzi complimented the squad for such an important victory, but remained low-key about Buffon's prodigy. 'That's what he gets paid to do,' Tanzi said. 'And what he makes should be enough for him even to stop Ronaldo's penalty shots.'

Empoli v Parma
March 15 1998

With the victory over Inter, Parma could begin to dream again. If not about the *scudetto*, at least about the Champions League. They had ten games remaining, and it would take about eight victories. Not easy in Serie A, and given their ups and downs, they would probably be lucky to get away with six victories and four draws. But with a little luck, everything was possible. They had now beaten 3rd-place Inter, and in the first half of the season tied the top two teams, Juventus and Lazio. What should Ancelotti's little army fear?

Certainly not Empoli. The team from Tuscany, which was sometimes in A, sometimes in B, certainly should not have caused problems for Parma. True, Ancelotti's boys were playing away, but it was not like playing against Inter at San Siro, or even Fiorentina. This was 15th-placed Empoli, who were fast heading for Serie B unless they got their act together.

Empoli had a roster of no-names, guys no one outside of Italy (and most within the country) have never heard of. They have names like Baldini, Bianconi, Fusco and Ficini, not exactly the line-up of the national team. And yet, Empoli have a shrewd manager, Luciano Spaletti, who runs the side well, and knows how to create difficulties for good teams. Later in the season, a referee's error would rob them of a goal against Juventus that might have changed the course of the championship.

But against Parma there were no charges of theft, no terrible calls, just a squad that was a little sleepy. *Corriere della Sera* called Parma 'unrecognizable', and they were, at least for part of the game. 'It wasn't a case of physical tiredness,' Ancelotti said, 'given that we played better in the second half.' But mentally, Parma weren't there, and after they fell behind 2–0, there was nothing to do. That was how it would end.

Not even Parma's once-vaunted defence, world-class players like Cannavaro and Thuram, were the same. Anyone can have a bad game, but these guys had a bad week. On Thursday, they let their chances for the Italian Cup slip away, and four days later they lost to a team that was fourth from the bottom of the pack. Parma slipped into 6th place, and once again Ancelotti's job suddenly didn't look so very sure.

At Empoli Cannavaro and Thuram, who are capable of shutting down Ronaldo, Bierhoff or Batistuta, were guilty of making bad passes and getting back to late too cover Empoli's strikers. The Mister blamed the bad game on psychological, not physical, tiredness. His keeper agreed. 'We needed to go into this game with the knife clenched between our teeth, and we failed to do that,' Buffon said.

Calisto Tanzi summed up the season as 'pretty negative' up until this point. 'After we got knocked out of the Cups, we played pretty badly,' the owner said. While he claimed that the decision regarding Ancelotti's future would be made by his son, he made it clear that the negative trend could only continue so long. 'I've already said that if we lost everything, he could draw his own conclusions,' insisted Tanzi, repeating almost word for word what he had told *La Gazzetta dello Sport*. 'The fact is that a lot of people are opposed to Ancelotti at this time – perhaps unjustly.'

What were Parma missing this season? Tanzi didn't want to respond. 'You have to ask the Mister that,' he said. 'If you ask the fans, some say it's a striker, some say midfield, others the defence. Certainly they're missing some conviction. We won the big matches, with Milan at home and with Inter at home, and played pretty well against Juventus. Then we lost some incredible games, like Brescia and Empoli. Empoli was just a disaster.'

Parma v Juventus
March 22 1998

In the 25th game of the regular season, Juventus showed why they were on top of the standings, and how they have won more *scudetti* than any other Italian squad. More than skill and speed, both of which they have in abundance, Juve have character. No matter that they lost their best defender, Ciro Ferrara, who broke his leg in the first game of the return leg. No matter that they sold their top scorer, Christian Vieri, for top dollars in Spain (Atlético Madrid got their money's worth, with Vieri's 20 goals in his first 21 games).

Admittedly, Juventus didn't look great in the first half against Parma; there were lapses in defence, as Parma scored two goals.

Mario Stanic headed one in on a free-kick, Massimo Crippa knocked in a corner, and Juve found themselves going into the dressing room 2–0 down. But they came out another team.

They made two substitutions immediately: Alessio Tacchinardi for Didier Deschamps in midfield, and midfielder Angelo Di Livio for defender Alessandro Birindelli. Ten minutes into the second half Tacchinardi put the ball in an empty net as Gigi Buffon got caught out of position, and five minutes later he gave a perfect pass to Filippo Inzaghi, who earned his weekly pay with a perfect diagonal ball that beat Buffon. It ended 2–2, but it might as well have been a victory for Juventus; they earned a point and managed to remain in 1st place.

Lippi looked like a genius. He sent Tacchinardi into the game, and boom, boom, one goal and one assist. But part of the problem was Parma; they lost concentration, and failed to dominate as they had in the first half. Buffon erred on the first Juve goal, and Parma were missing Dino Baggio, their midfield stopper, and a former Juventino, who was out with a stretched muscle. But above all it was Juventus, with 1st place riding on the outcome of the game, who were determined not to let it slip away. And that's Juventus; they might not win all their games, but they hardly ever lose the important ones.

For all their problems, Parma could hardly complain. Yes, they should have won and picked up an important three points in the standings. Instead, they settled for a single point and remained tied for 5th place with Roma, and 9 points behind Juve. But in two matches with Juventus this season they had drawn both, having let leads slip. Back in the autumn, Ancelotti had been satisfied with his team, but in March he was angry for having let it slip away. 'We're in danger of making this the season of regrets,' he said. 'There have been too many times that we've played well and then thrown away our good efforts.'

Juve coach Marcello Lippi had just proven why many believe him the best coach in Italy: a decisive 4–1 Champions League victory at Kiev; now a 2–2 come-from-behind point at Parma, all in the same week. Lippi's tactical changes against Parma turned out to be perfect, but he gave all the credit to his players, saying it was time to build them a monument in Turin.

But was this the same Juve that had only managed a draw with last-place Napoli two weeks earlier? 'Nothing can be taken for granted in the Italian championship,' Lippi insisted. 'Beginning with the matches that on paper look like they're the easiest. Before the game against Naples, a lot of people pointed out that there were 40 points separating the two teams. And I pleaded with the players not to make the same error. The fact of the matter is that you can draw against Piacenza or Napoli and not even have too many good excuses.'

11 Juventus, the Team with 10 Million Supporters

At newsstands and tobacco shops in downtown Milan, there's a rather curious postcard for sale. It's a photo of the inside of San Siro, packed to the brim. There's a black and white border on the sides, and black and white letters at the top, '*Forza Magica Juve*' (Go Magical Juventus). What do Juventus have to do with San Siro? Nothing at all. They play there once a year. The fact is that Juventus sells. They have 1200 Juve clubs spread throughout the country, with 600,000 members and countless other faithful followers. The tobacco shops also offer the exact same postcard, but with red and black borders, and the exhortation, '*Forza Magico Milan*'. It probably doesn't sell as well.

Juventus, who are owned by Italy's first family, the Agnellis, celebrated their 100th anniversary in style during the 1996–97 season, winning the Italian league championship, the Inter-Continental Cup and the Super Cup. They were favoured to win the Champions League, but Borussia Dortmund outplayed them and outscored them 3–1.

The following season wasn't quite as brilliant, but Juve usually won when they needed to. They lost in the semi-final of the Italian Cup to Lazio, but played as if they didn't really want to win. In the second leg coach Marcello Lippi kept a half dozen starters at home. Juventus were clearly more interested in the *scudetto* and the Champions League than the tiny Italian Cup.

In Serie A, they took over 1st place from Inter at mid-season, and despite threats from Lazio, stayed there until the very end. In the Champions League, they thrashed Dynamo Kiev 4–1 in the return match to go to the semi-finals against Monaco, who they also beat handily: the first match finished 4–1, making the return something of a formality.

Juventus, known as 'La Signora' (the Lady), is to football what the New York Times is to journalism: elegant, refined, sometimes boring, but above all solid. Even the classic black and white striped home jerseys give Juve a bit of the grey look. La Signora has 25 Italian league championships to her credit, more than any other team in the country. And while she can boast about outstanding players – Michel Platini, Roberto Baggio, and, more recently, Gianluca Vialli and Fabrizio Ravanelli – during the past few years coach Marcello Lippi has gone out of his way not to let the squad depend on two or three players. Anybody is dispensable; anybody can be substituted, or sold.

The team's management shares the same policy; when Vialli and Ravanelli got better offers in England, Juve let them go. Borussia Dortmund, Juve's opponents in the 1997 Champions League Final, had five former Juventini on their squad, including the midfield duo of Andy Möeller and Paulo Sousa. As long as the team wins, the fans seem to accept the loss of their favourite players, some of whom are incredibly talented. They are Italy's most popular team, and have been for decades.

An estimated 10 million people in Italy, or one out of every three males (men, boys and infants), root for Juve. The squad may have as many as 10 million fans abroad as well, giving it more followers than a number of national teams. Juve is especially strong in the southern half of Italy, which lacks serious teams in A. They also picked up a few million new fans in the 1960s when poor southerners moved to Turin to work at Fiat and the other factories.

Juventus realize, more than most Italian squads, the importance of turnover. 'They've put together a wide range of players who are all good, and, without any sentimental attachment, have substituted those who are getting older or aren't in top physical condition,' says Giorgio Tosatti, columnist for the Milan daily Corriere della Sera, and one of the country's foremost football experts. Recently they sold pony-tailed Baggio (always a crowd pleaser) to Milan, then let Ravanelli and Vialli go to England.

Juventus used to win and not worry about how much money they spent. Under Umberto Agnelli, Gianni's brother, however, they have put their books back into shape. They have proven that they can win and save at the same time. Juve's top scorer in the '96–97 season was a young striker just reaching his prime, Christian Vieri. Despite initial management claims that he would remain with the squad at all costs, that changed when Atlético Madrid came up with 34 billion lire (nearly £12 million) for the youngster. Everyone at the team is on the market. And yet, they still keep winning.

Juve's average age is low, which means the athletic preparation is high. 'They run a lot more than the others,' Tosatti says. 'And they do this because they have the possibility of substituting players who are tired or injured with others who are at about the same level.' Not a lot of teams can do that. Juve are young, but above all they have strength in depth. Moreno Torricelli, an experienced international, spent most of the season on Juve's bench, as did Uruguayan striker Daniel Fonseca and midfielder Antonio Conte. Angelo Di Livio, another Italian national, was also frequently a substitute after the arrival of Edgar Davids, who became part of an overpowering midfield that also included the French Connection, Didier Deschamps and Zinedine Zidane.

Despite the influx of foreign stars in recent years in Italian football, Juventus are built primarily around Italians or Europeans who have already played in Italy, and know the system and the language well. They have only two Latin Americans, defender Paolo Montero and striker Daniel Fonseca. 'Above all, it's an Italian-French team, and they are very united,' Tosatti says. 'It's a lot harder to train players and get everyone to understand if you have seven or eight players from different countries.' Witness Milan.

Tosatti considers goalkeeper Angelo Peruzzi 'the best in the world' and also gives high marks to the defence, especially veteran Ciro Ferrara and Montero. The attack has produced goals; if not in abundance then enough to keep them near the top of the league. Alessandro Del Piero has been the game-maker, and Zinedine Zidane and Filippo Inzaghi score when it becomes necessary. Inzaghi scored three goals against Dynamo Kiev – in Kiev – in the Champions League.

Juventus have the ability to do without stars, which is odd for a top squad in Italy. That's not to say Alessandro Del Piero is not a star (he's occasionally brilliant) but they don't need goal-scoring machines. They didn't even go after Ronaldo, although they have shown interest in Udinese's German bomber, Oliver Bierhoff.

The team lost only one regular season match in the 1996–97 season, 0–1 against Parma, and much of the credit goes to the defence. 'They had serious injuries to four starting players, but found the right substitute every time,' notes Gianni Mura of the Rome daily *La Repubblica*. 'That means they don't just train eleven players, but eighteen, and have them all ready.'

With the exception of their loss in the Champions League Final to Borussia, the 1996–97 season was almost perfect. They made Eric Cantona and his mates at Manchester United look like a bunch of schoolboys in an early Cup-tie in England. They also had important victories in the regular season, such as a 6–1 thrashing of rival AC Milan at San Siro. But they clinched the league championship in a much humbler way, with a 1–1 draw with Atalanta in Bergamo.

It was the first goal of the season for Mark Iuliano, a full-back, just another of the twenty-two players on the roster. All very *Juventine*. 'This is a team in which everyone helps one another,' Mura says. 'No one tries to be the star. Maybe because they've seen what happens with the stars. They get sold.'

Coach Marcello Lippi is adamant about that. 'No prima donna, no privileges,' he says. 'If a player doesn't agree with that he can walk.' Some Juve fans have criticized Lippi and the management for a lack of billboard attractions in the squad, but the coach will hear nothing of it: 'You might even like the antics and the caprice of a champion, but I believe the people appreciate more things like humility and intelligence.' And willpower. Midfielder Didier

Deschamps gives credit to Lippi and the extraordinary unity of the team, which on paper looks no stronger than either AC Milan or Inter. 'We just want it more,' says Deschamps.

Ancelotti agrees. 'What they have is a winning mentality,' he says. 'There's a desire to fight for every ball, and never let up, even though these guys have won everything there is to win in the last few years.' Parma's Mister thinks Juventus are the best team in Europe, and probably the best in the world. 'I wish we had what they had,' he said, adding that he wasn't sure what that magical element was that gave them unity and determination. 'Part of it's the history of the club, and pride in playing for them, but there's something more than that as well.'

Lilian Thuram considers the encounters with Juve the most challenging matches of the season. 'The nice thing about playing against them is that you don't have to make any effort to concentrate,' he says. 'You know that you're facing the best team in the world. All the words and all the advice really aren't worth anything.'

Juve were a supersquad long before the era of supersquads in Italy, and abroad; they supplied nine players to the national team that went to the World Cup in Argentina in 1978 (and finished fourth). More impressively, six *Juventini* started on the team that won the World Cup in Spain four years later: Dino Zoff in goal; Claudio Gentile, Antonio Cabrini, Gaetano Scirea, Marco Tardelli, and the hero of the games, Paolo Rossi, in attack. Ancelotti considers Scirea his favourite player from the past; he liked his style of play, and even more his attitude, humble and hard-working. Scirea was later killed in a car accident in Poland while on a scouting assignment for Juventus.

Juve's fans have grown accustomed to winning. They have more *scudetti* (25) than any other team in Serie A. Milan follows at a distance with 15, while Inter has won 13. Four of Milan's *scudetti* are from this decade, and the traditional Italian powerhouse match-up has been Juventus–Inter. In international competitions, Juve have won every other major title at least once. Unfortunately,

117

their name will always be connected with a game they played in May of 1985. It was the first Champions Cup victory for Juve, but a bitter one indeed. Hooligan violence left 38 people dead, mostly Juve fans, at the match in the Heysel Stadium, Belgium.

The Champions League has become a kind of cross for Juve. Although they won in 1996 – but only on penalty kicks – against Ajax, they lost to Borussia Dortmund the following year 3–1. And this season, they once again went into the Final as the favourites, but Real Madrid sneaked away with a 1–0 victory in a disappointing match. What happened? The team Ancelotti believes to be 'the best in the world' played well for 15 minutes and then disappeared. Edgar Davids played well in midfield for the black and whites, although he missed his only chance for a goal, and everyone else was apparently worn out from the race for the *scudetto*. There were celebrations in Italy, however. Inter and Lazio supporters, happy to see their nemesis finally defeated, partied into the early hours of the morning.

Although they struggled early on in the Champions League, and came close to elimination, Juventus normally play so well in key games that some people have suggested the players were taking illegal drugs before the big matches. Unlikely, but they do normally know how to save their energies for when they're most needed. And despite their dominance in the last few years, they also know what they don't have to win.

The 1965 Inter and 1994 Milan squads remain the only Italian sides to have won the 'double' *scudetto* and Champions League.

Not even Ronaldo could bring Inter the *scudetto*, but if you believe the conspiracy theories, that wasn't his fault. 'I don't think the refs' mistakes that favoured Juventus were just a coincidence,' said Ruben Razzante, 28, a rabid Inter supporter who teaches law at the Catholic University of Milan. 'Juventus were still celebrating their 100th anniversary when the season also saw the death of one of their biggest supporters, Giovannino "Little Gianni" Agnelli,' Razzante pointed out.

Giovannino, 33, the son of Juventus president Umberto Agnelli and nephew of former Fiat chief Gianni Agnelli, died in December of a rare stomach cancer. He passionately loved Juve, and saw them against Manchester United just a few days before he died. Several Juve players dedicated the season to Giovannino after his death. But was that reason enough for the powers that be to rig the championship? Razzante thinks so. 'They really didn't want Inter, in their first year with Ronaldo, to win it,' he said. 'They did everything possible to have it decided early and let the Italians prepare for the World Cup.'

Conspiracy theories aside, Razzante is the first to admit that Juve fielded a spectacular squad this season. 'I was there for Inter–Juventus in January,' he said. 'We should have lost 3–0, and instead we won 1–0 by a goal from Djorkaeff. But Juve were a perfect machine. It's a great team and Lippi's the best manager in Italy. They shouldn't need help.' Razzante doesn't believe Juve can get 'help' every year. A true fan, he believes Inter is at the beginning of a long domination of Serie A. 'We're not tremendously strong, but we're cynical,' he said. 'It's old-style [defensive] Italian football. Not particularly pretty, but it works.'

12 Money and Markets

To hear Andrea Kerbaker talk, Pirelli and Ronaldo were a match made in heaven – or was it Brazil? The director of communications for Pirelli Tyres and Cables couldn't be happier about the boy from Brazil. The company began sponsoring Inter in 1995, the same year in which Massimo Moratti bought it back from Ernesto Pellegrini. A year later, Pirelli jumped from mere sponsor to part-ner, as the company purchased 13 per cent of the team.

Moratti's father had owned the team three decades ago, and saw it win two European Cups in the 60s. The Morattis and the Pirellis are old Milanese families, and both the company and the team had gone through a difficult period in the early 1990s, during which they had laid the groundwork ready for a comeback. Pirelli had made strides in the field of fibre optics, gaining a strong foothold in telecommunications, and Inter had already finished 3rd in the league the second season after Moratti Jr. bought the club. Now they were in the running for the championship, and Kerbaker was pleasantly amused that die-hard fans wore hats that bore the name of the sponsor, not the team.

For many reasons it seemed that Inter were right for Pirelli, and vice versa, Kerbaker explained, pointing to the friendship be-tween Moratti and the dashing young chairman of Pirelli, Marco Tronchetti Provera. But, above all, it was a dollars and cents decision. 'Cables don't need a lot of advertising,' Kerbaker said. 'But tyres are another story. The target we have for our advertising is male, 25–54, and that's exactly the same target as football.' Women don't seem to figure. 'If a woman goes to buy tyres, she'll tell them to put on what she already has or to do whatever they want, or to make a suggestion,' Kerbaker says. 'But she won't say she wants one brand over another. Men, on the other hand, know what they want when it comes to tyres.'

Serious drivers consider Pirelli a sporty tyre, and although the company has not been involved with Formula One racing since the 1950s, polls they've done reveal that about 25 per cent of the people think they are. Such is their reputation as a good, fast tyre. The company has been involved in rugby and volleyball sponsorship, and is the technical supplier for the Subaru rally team. Football was new to them, but they found it quite enticing. 'Not only did the target [market] coincide with football, but football was right for the sporty image,' Kerbaker says. In advertising campaigns emphasizing speed and sport, or as they call it, 'power and control', Pirelli have used American sprinter Carl Lewis, and more recently the French Olympian Marie-Jo Perec.

And then there was the Brazil connection. About 30 per cent of Pirelli's turnover comes from Brazil, and the tyres and cables producer is the fourth largest industrial group in the country. 'There's a lot of synergy that will come out of this,' noted Kerbaker, as an assistant in the office next door assembled a mountain of clips from Monday's papers, each with the Pirelli logo clearly visible on the Inter jersey. 'It's a coincidence that makes us happy,' Kerbaker said. 'Ronaldo was particularly interesting to Pirelli. There will be a lot of things possible that wouldn't be possible with a Russian player, for example.' But Kerbaker insisted that it was only a coincidence, and that it was Moratti, and not the Pirelli company, that pushed so hard for the Phenomenon.

Kerbaker's office makes an attempt at measuring the impact of its sponsorship, at least in Italy. Every time the logo is clearly readable, either on television or in the press, they record it. For example, 20 seconds at 20:30 on Rai Uno. Or page 27 of *Corriere della Sera*, 1/8 of a page. Then they calculate what the same spot would have cost them in direct advertising. For 1996–1997, the discounted advertising rate came to about 20 billion lire (£7 million). 'And think that we paid 4 billion lire (£1.4 million) for that,' Kerbaker said with a smile. 'This is our return on investment. It speaks for itself.' And that doesn't include anything in the foreign

121

markets, although Inter's games are seen in Asia, Latin America and the US. In the first three months after Ronaldo came, the coverage was already up 57 per cent from the same period the year before. Of course it's indirect advertising, but it's still extremely powerful, and ends up in some places where traditional advertising won't. The entire front page of *L'Equipe* in France, for example. That's not for sale.

'We are very lucky because Ronaldo's such a nice boy – and he's really only a boy,' Kerbaker mused. Maradona wasn't particularly nice, and was always getting into trouble. Not the kind of guy you'd want your company to be associated with. Pirelli has the same feeling with Ronaldo that it had with Carl Lewis. Very balanced, somewhat low key. Not someone who's going to say or do anything stupid. In other words, not Mike Tyson and not Eric Cantona.

But why football and not Formula One, with its 600 million viewers worldwide? What could be better for a sporty image than auto racing? 'There are good reasons to be in, and good reasons to be out,' Kerbaker answered. 'It's very expensive, and if you want to be in Formula One, you have to be a protagonist, and that's not easy. Until last year it was only Goodyear. Now it's Goodyear and Bridgestone, but all the other tyre makers are divided about whether they should be in or not.' Winning is everything in Formula One, and in auto racing the product actually makes a difference.

'No one is going to think Pirelli stinks because Inter is losing, but with racing it's different,' Kerbaker remarked. 'It's very important that you win.' And though it's much less important in football, Pirelli is clearly going to be happy if Inter can provide it with not only a sporty but also a winning image. Ronaldo should be able to help them do that.

Football in Italy used to be seen largely as a recreation for very rich people (many of them not so smart) or for the social promotion of some other fairly wealthy folks who were involved in rather dubious affairs. A handful of different Milan owners were either arrested or fled the country before they could be in the decades before Berlusconi took over the red and blacks. Whether old money or new money, football was mostly a family affair, and a kind of side business, one that was expected to lose money.

In fact, the squads weren't even allowed to make a profit for their owners. Until the law recently changed, clubs had to be registered as non-profit enterprises. Not that many of them were in a position to make money. Except for the biggest and wealthiest clubs – most notably Juventus – ownership frequently changed as the debts mounted. And even the Agnelli family has now stopped subsidizing Juve as the squad has gotten its books in order.

'Now it's become a real business,' said Lanfranco Vaccari of *La Gazzetta dello Sport*. 'So what's the problem? On the one hand, you have a structure that culturally isn't ready for it, and on the other, an extraordinary amount of money coming in from television and sponsorship.' Vaccari sees the rush to the stock market as a dangerous trend at this point. 'Football teams in Italy don't own their stadiums; they don't produce anything; what do they have?' he asks. 'They used to have the *cartellino* [the card] of the players, and then the Bosman ruling took that away. So what's a football team in Italy? An owner with a lot of money.'

Vaccari sees a host of problems for stock-market listings of clubs. 'What exactly are you selling if your only assets are your TV money and your players?' he asks. 'Why should I invest? Because you have Ronaldo? This is terrifying.' While English clubs make a killing on merchandising rights, the Italians haven't been able to get this aspect of their game together, for a number of different reasons. The league counts for almost nothing in dealing with the clubs. They're still behind on television rights, and have failed to bring the squads together to make an official line of jerseys. Most kits sold are fake replicas.

Not that they'd earn as much off the shirts as in England or Germany, but they'd make something. 'Italians have this thing about dressing well, and most fans would never even think about going to the stadium in a jersey,' said Marco Trabucchi, a Milan-based agent for several hockey players, and an avid football fan.

'You go to see Borussia Dortmund play and half the stadium is yellow. Here you put on a yellow or a red shirt, and people think you're crazy.'

For years, Italian owners ran their clubs capriciously, or as a way of gaining acceptance into the top levels of the financial world. It was worth whatever it cost. But the football business has become a kind of show business – witness Nike's deal with the Brazilian national team to have them play nine games in 1997–98 as part of the 'Brazil World Tour'.

As a result, there were major conflicts between the Brazilians and the Italian clubs who didn't want to lose some of their best players for Nike matches on the other side of the globe that meant nothing except exposure for Nike. 'Football has became a global spectacle, but FIFA hasn't caught on yet,' Vaccari said. 'They need to organize the schedules so there won't be these conflicts.' Ronaldo, anxious to get some rest, would certainly agree.

The economy in Italy divides the country between north and south, and that division extends also to football. The top half of the boot, wealthy and industrial, continues to produce the best squads, and the teams from Milan and Turin have won more *scudetti* than all the other cities combined. (In addititon to the big three northern clubs, Turin's 'other' squad, Torino, have 7 to their credit.

At the other end of the the country, the biggest club (from the largest city) in Sicily, Palermo, spends most of its time in Serie C, along with teams such as Gualdo and Nocerina. Lecce and Bari, who hate each other, celebrate wildly if they manage to stay in Serie A. Bari pulled it off respectably this year, finishing 11th, but Lecce got sent down. Naples is the only team from the south to have won the *scudetto* in Serie A. With the help of Diego Maradona, they took the title twice, in 1987 and 1990. Napoli had money to spend then, and were closely linked with the powerful Christian Democratic party, or the DC, which dominated Italy for most of the post-war period.

Maradona left, the DC crumbled under the 'Clean Hands' corruption investigations of the early 1990s, and the banks shut the taps. The club found themselves loaded with debt and started selling many of their best players. Gianfranco Zola, Fabio Cannavaro and Massimo Crippa ended up at Parma; forward Daniel Fonseca was sold to Roma for about $10 million, although the Uruguayan would later move on to Juventus.

Napoli won only two games all season in '97–98, both of them at home, 2–1 against Empoli and 2–0 against Vicenza. The supporters at San Paolo saw 11 losses and 4 draws in the squad's most disappointing season in their ninety-year history. By mid-season, the squad was already on its third manager, still going nowhere, and the supporters had seen enough. After losing 0–4 at home to Parma in December, fires broke out in several parts of the stadium as angry *tifosi* registered their displeasure with the squad by burning the plastic seats. The fires produced a lot of black smoke and a foul smell, but didn't do anything for Napoli's level of play.

The more rabid *tifosi* then fought with the police and gathered outside the home of the team's owner, Corrado Ferlaino, in a loud display of disgust. Other Neapolitans expressed their displeasure with the ownership more discreetly, calling for Ferlaino to sell the squad to the residents of the city. A nice idea, but not very practical. Luciano De Crescenzo, a well-known writer from Naples, didn't lose his sense of humour over the disaster of Napoli. He invited Berlusconi to buy the club, 'then he can give us all the players he doesn't use at Milan'.

Cannavaro, who started as a ballboy with Napoli in the glory days of Maradona, watched their fall into Serie B with genuine compassion. It appeared already clear after only about ten games that nothing, not even Maradona's return, was going to save Napoli. Some thirteen new players were bought since the start of the season, for about £12.5 million, but they didn't make much of a difference. Relegation to Serie B became mathematically certain after the 29th game of the season, played just before Easter. Parma–Napoli ended 3–1 and Cannavaro walked off the field consoling goalkeeper Giuseppe Taglialatela. Both were in tears.

Football players don't cry every Sunday, and the emotional scene made all the television highlights and the sports pages of the papers the next day. Yet there was something completely logical about Napoli's relegation to B. Naples is a southern city, and the south of Italy doesn't produce powerful teams. It was a near miracle that Napoli had managed to stay in A for so long.

13 April, or How Ancelotti Lost His Job

Ancelotti had hoped to be in the running for the *scudetto* by spring, but instead he found himself struggling to keep his job. The last match of March, a 2–2 draw away with Roma, was at least respectable. His boys came back from a 2–0 deficit, and in any case Parma had earned a point and remained among the top six teams, in the all-important UEFA zone.

On April 5 Parma hosted Fiorentina, who despite the mood swings of their owner, Vittorio Cecchi Gori, had been playing pretty good football. They had a great Latin American attacking trident, with Gabriele Batistuta, the Brazilian-turned-Belgian A.L. Oliveira and Edmundo, back from *Carnevale* in Brazil and now on his best behaviour, scoring a goal the week before.

The Animal helped ruin Ancelotti's day, week, month and maybe his season. Ultimately, not his career, but the damage was done for the 1997–98 championship. Edmundo scored one goal and delivered a beautiful, generous assist for the winner as Parma fell 1–2. The home fans made their displeasure known as never before. Several waited for Ancelotti after the game, calling for his resignation.

But Ancelotti has developed a thick skin after twenty years in Serie A. The jeers didn't bother him nearly as much as the failure to pick up three points. Parma remained with 46 points and fell out of 6th place, losing at least temporarily their ticket into UEFA. Fiorentina, whose first-year coach Alberto Malesani also had to make UEFA in order to keep his job, took their spot.

That was the beginning of the end for Ancelotti at Parma, or so it seemed. The week before Easter was also Passion Week for Mister Ancelotti, who was going to suffer more in a few days than he had in his previous two years with the club. Here's what happened:

Friday April 3
Ancelotti meets with Tanzi Jr. and they talk about possible players to pick up for the following season.

Sunday April 5
Parma, playing at home, lose to Fiorentina 1−2. Ancelotti is jeered by the fans − not the Boys and the other feisty young ones from the *curva*, but the older ones who sit in the good seats. Tanzi Sr. takes the loss badly and sees it as an invitation to go shopping for a new manager.

Monday April 6
Calisto Tanzi sends an emissary to make contact with Malesani in Florence. Ancelotti believes Tanzi, father and son, are working on their own, without consulting other members of the team's executive board.

Tuesday April 7
Stefano Tanzi meets with the entire coaching staff. Ancelotti feels neither reassured nor encouraged by the tone of the encounter. Tanzi Jr. stresses the need to reach the UEFA Cup. Ancelotti has the distinct sense that the president is interested in the future of the club, but no longer sees Ancelotti as a part of it. 'It wasn't a discussion about the long-term, because, essentially, they don't believe in what I've done,' Ancelotti says, with resignation.

The Mister meets with the team on the same day, encouraging his players to finish the season well and make the UEFA Cup. He tells them about his encounter with Stefano Tanzi.

Thursday April 9

The rumour begins circulating that Parma have made contact with Malesani. 'In a way I was waiting for it, but what was surprising was that it leaked out and everybody was talking about it,' Ancelotti said. 'This caused a lot of tension among the squad. It really wasn't harmful for me but for the entire team.' And yet it would do damage to Ancelotti. After a splendid career as a player, and a promising first year as a manager in Serie A, he was about to get fired. And everyone would soon be in on the secret.

Friday April 10

Good Friday. The cat's out of the bag. The top story in *La Gazzetta dello Sport* runs under the headline, MALESANI'S GOING TO PARMA. Calisto Tanzi shows up at the Hotel Toscanini, where the squad is staying before the game, which will be on Saturday in order to avoid playing on Easter Sunday. Tanzi denies that any agreement has been reached, and repeats that no decision will be made until the end of the season. But what was telling was what Tanzi didn't say: never once did he deny that there had been contact made with Malesani.

Ancelotti understands at this point that after two seasons in Serie A, his story with Parma has ended. 'If Malesani is backing away from Bologna, with whom he had already planned what players they were going to get for next year, he's really naïve, unless he has a piece of paper in hand from Parma,' Ancelotti said. 'And yet, I don't think everything is black and white yet. Maybe there's been a kind of handshake deal.'

Saturday April 11

Parma, with two goals from Crespo, beat last-place Napoli 3–1. Ancelotti and his players have two days of rest, Easter Sunday and Monday.

★   ★   ★

Malesani had also been courted by Bologna, and was, along with Alberto Zaccheroni of Udinese, a kind of 'manager of the moment', someone with a strong reputation at a good but not great squad who had bigger ambitions. Literally speaking, Tanzi may have been telling the truth when he told the players no decision had been made – that is, if Malesani had not yet signed – but a coach has got to be lined up before the summer so a club knows what they're looking for in the players' market.

If Ancelotti did get the axe – and he was 95 per cent sure he was going to after Passion Week – he wasn't going to be getting any offers from big clubs in May, who would have all come up with their solutions. The good news was that he had a three-year contract, and could 'study up' for a year and still get paid for it. Maybe he would even learn English, he thought. The situation could have been worse.

The irony about Malesani going to Parma was that in many ways he was similar to Ancelotti: young, and still untested in Serie A. What was more ironic after the news broke was that Fiorentina, who had looked so good beating Parma at Tardini, drew their next game and lost the next two after that. In the meantime Parma registered three victories, picked up nine points and were suddenly looking decidedly better than Fiorentina for a UEFA place.

With three games left to play in the regular season, Parma were in 4th place with 55 points on the heels of a suddenly struggling Lazio, while Fiorentina were down in 7th place with just 48 points. Malesani, manager of the moment a month ago, had suddenly lost some of his lustre. And yet, if he had told Bologna he was no longer interested, that was only because he had a firm offer in hand from Parma. Or was it so firm? Even a signed piece of paper, if it hasn't been deposited with the league, is worth virtually nothing.

The Tanzis, father and son, found themselves in a very uncomfortable position. While they had stated publicly that they wouldn't make any decision on a new manager until the end of the season, that's virtually impossible to do. By the middle of May, when the *campionato* is all wrapped up, there are no good managers available. In early April the Tanzis had reached at least a handshake deal with Malesani.

A column on April 26 in the nation's leading paper, *Corriere della Sera*, further aggravated the situation for the Tanzi family. Running under the headline IMPROVISATION IS IN POWER, the column took to task three owners: Tanzi, Cecchi Gori and Giuseppe Gazzoni of Bologna. 'You can't say that clarity is what presides in the programmes of some of the most important clubs in our championship,' wrote Giancarlo Padovan. The Tanzis, he said, will not be able to remain faithful to their commitment to confirm Ancelotti as manager, which Calisto Tanzi had stated and repeated publicly.

Padovan didn't find that surprising, given the curious Asprilla re-purchase from England. 'From executives who are capable of spending 18 billion lire (£6 million) for Tino Asprilla and his multiple injuries . . . one can expect a wide gamma of behaviour.' He accused the Tanzis of acting capriciously, just like Cecchi Gori. 'They change ideas from one Sunday to the next,' he wrote. 'First they support Ancelotti, then it's enough for them to lose at home with Malesani's Fiorentina to go shopping for Malesani.' Padovan was, perhaps, a little harsh, but he was correct. Parma's top brass had found themselves in a managerial mess.

Stefano Tanzi, who speaks only rarely with the press, talked to reporters on the day of the *Corriere* column, which appeared on the same Sunday Parma were playing Lazio in Rome. Stefano countered the attack of improvisation. 'Parma have won three Cups in seven years, finished 2nd and went to the Champions League last season,' Stefano said. 'Asprilla? He's worth a lot, and you'll see that very soon, maybe in the World Cup. Bringing him back to Parma wasn't a mistake. He'll show himself to be very useful next season.'

The only consolation the Tanzis had was that they weren't the only ones that *Corriere* attacked. Padovan also went after Cecchi Gori for his indecision about Malesani. Fiorentina's owner was initially against keeping the young coach, then changed his mind.

Bologna's Gazzoni got beaten up for first telling his popular manager, Renzo Ulivieri, that he should be looking for a new team, and then trying to keep him after he lost Malesani to Parma.

At the end of April it was still difficult to see who the winners and losers were in the game of musical chairs played by the managers. Malesani looked like he was headed for Parma. Ulivieri looked like he was headed for Naples, who were definitely headed for Serie B. Trapattoni looked like he was headed for Fiorentina, and Ancelotti looked like he was about to be one of the best-paid unemployed football managers in the country.

Ancelotti may have been about to lose his post, but he wasn't going to fret too much over the Tanzi family's troubles. After the April 5 crisis, losing at home to Fiorentina, his squad had registered three straight victories. The 3–1 victory over Napoli was not a surprise, nor the 0–2 win at Lecce. But Ancelotti also pulled off a come-from-behind victory in Rome against third-place Lazio, who had been one of the hottest teams for much of the season, and who would eventually win the Italian Cup.

It was an important win that showed once again that Ancelotti and his boys could play with the best. In fact, against the top three teams – Juventus, Inter and Lazio – Parma only lost once in six games during the season (1–0 at Inter). They beat Inter by the same score at Parma (when Buffon stopped a penalty shot by Ronaldo); they drew with Juventus twice; and they drew one match and won the other with Lazio.

Ancelotti believes mental toughness is what makes it possible for Parma to play well against the better teams. Sharp, focused minds means sharp passing and no stupid mistakes. He ruefully recalls a Sunday in his first season at Parma in which, in the middle of a positive run, they lost to Napoli. The problem, the Mister insists, was concentration. 'I could tell at lunch and by the way they were talking on the bus that they weren't concentrated,' he said. 'I would have paid anything at that moment to have called off the match and played it on another day.'

The games with Napoli and Lecce meant something special for

Ancelotti this season. Players and staff alike were all nervous about the future, and the owners had clearly lost faith in their manager. The fans were split. The older ones in the *tribuna* wanted Ancelotti out. The *curva*, who had often jeered Ancelotti and Crespo earlier in the season, wanted him to stay. The main fans' club, the Boys, would later release a statement expressing their solidarity with Carletto.

Against Napoli, Hernán Crespo showed what a gentleman he is twice in the course of about 30 seconds. Crespo, playing in attack with the tiny Brazilian Bolzan Adailton, normally a substitute, watched as his team-mate beat the Napoli keeper and shot diagonally from about 15 metres out. Crespo, standing at the mouth of the goal, waited to see if the ball was going to enter, in order to let Adailton get his third goal of the season. When he saw it wouldn't make it, he flicked it in, picking up his twelfth goal of the campaign. For all the jeers he had taken from the fans, he was still Parma's top scorer, and a generous guy as well.

Crespo then ran immediately to give Ancelotti a big bear hug. 'He stuck with me through the tough times this season,' Crespo said later. 'It was right for me to show that I was with him now that he was in trouble.' Unfortunately, the goal against Napoli would be Crespo's last of the season. He pulled a muscle in the following game, and didn't play again. At that point even the World Cup became a question mark for the young Argentinian.

Against Lecce, Ancelotti received a similar show of solidarity. When Parma scored their first goal, actually a deflected Lecce own goal off a shot by Massimo Crippa, the entire Parma team went over to greet Ancelotti. You would have thought the team had won the *scudetto*. All they had done was taken a step closer to UEFA qualification. More importantly, their show of solidarity very eloquently put an end to rumours that the players weren't happy with Ancelotti's way of running the team. That was good news for the Mister, but made the situation somewhat more embarrassing for the Tanzis. Why get rid of a manager the team likes and respects?

'I think about 80 per cent of the players are on my side,' Ancel-

133

otti said. 'Some of those who are sitting on the bench might not be with me, but that's to be expected.' Ancelotti claimed he didn't feel betrayed by Parma. 'Absolutely not,' he said. 'That's football. I only hope we can clear up the situation as soon as possible. Confusion doesn't help a team remain calm and concentrated.'

The Mister understood the indecision of the owners, but argued that they shouldn't keep him or boot him on account of one Sunday's results. 'I might make UEFA from a shot that knocks off the post and goes in,' he said. 'But if that ball hits the post and then goes out, what happens then? They say that Ancelotti stinks? I don't think a great team can be judged only on the basis of its results, otherwise one Sunday you're in, and the next you're out.'

Ancelotti thought the victory over Lazio may have given him a chance to save face at Parma. 'I don't think the Parma guys know how to tell Malesani that they don't mean to keep the agreement,' the Mister said. 'That's what the rumours are, at least.'

Parma's fickle fans were also coming back to believe in Ancelotti. While the Boys had stood by him when the news about Malesani first broke, now some of the others were also coming to his defence. What were the team owners to tell them? That they had already made a deal for a new coach? April may not have been an easy month for Ancelotti, but in a way it was even worse for the Tanzis.

When Parma got knocked out of the Coppa Italia, Ancelotti said this was becoming 'the season of regrets', and he had some of his own. 'There are things I should have said, and I didn't, but I won't say them now either, because I don't want to create problems,' the Mister noted. 'In terms of players, I should have probably asked for some others. I pushed for only one, Guardiola from Barcelona, and we didn't get him.'

By the end of the month, Ancelotti had not spoken with Stefano Tanzi (or any of the other team executives) about the players' market since April 3. And unless they did talk about who to bring on the team, it meant it wasn't going to be Ancelotti's squad any longer. In any case, he thought they needed four or five new players. The team had already been negotiating for two of them, Argentinian midfielder Juan Sebastian Veron, who was at Sampdoria, and defender Michele Serena of Fiorentina.

14 Babes in Boysland: Football on Television

For all their football fever, Italians get to see very little of Serie A on television. One game a week, the only match held on Sunday night, is shown on cable. You can also subscribe to the cable company, Tele+, to follow one team each week, but you only get to see them when they're playing away.

There's also one tape-delayed game a week shown on public television, and some of the local stations will broadcast their team's Sunday game on Monday. That's what happens in Parma, for example.

But live coverage of Serie A on public television is non-existent. The result is that there's a tremendous amount of TV time talking about Milan, Inter, Juventus and the rest, but very little of Serie A itself. So millions of viewers settle for talk: some of it frivolous, some serious, some obnoxious.

The most obnoxious goes on air on Monday night. *Il Processo di Biscardi* (*Biscardi's Trial*) has been running for eighteen years. Aldo Biscardi hosts a crew of loudmouths who spend the best part of two hours shouting at each other. The loudest and most annoying of these is Maurizio Mosca, who does know something about football, but whose claim to fame as a journalist was an interview he 'invented'* with the great Zico of Brazil for *Gazzetta dello Sport*.

---

* Mosca defends the August 1983 interview as legitimate, even though he admits that it was culled from a section of the paper that collected questions from readers for different players. Mosca went to see Zico around August 10 and put the questions to him. Not all of the answers

Other guests are somewhat more restrained. Italo Cucci, the editor of the weekly magazine *Guerin Sportivo*, for example, or Xavier Jacobelli, the editor of *TuttoSport*. The women are also well behaved. One blonde who sits next to Biscardi has the job of calling timeout every so often for adverts. The second one, Caterina Collavati, the wife of a former *Juventino*, actually knows something about football. And the third, Irene Pivetti, gets invited because she's a parliamentarian and the former Speaker of the House. A supporter of Milan, Pivetti's not afraid to express her opinion, but she does know how to behave. Biscardi also brings in a fortune-teller for added excitement.

Mosca has the biggest mouth, but another one of the talking heads, Gino Menicucci, also displays excellent volume. When four or five get talking at the same time it's really quite a row. *Biscardi's Trial* is aired by Telemontecarlo, a network run by Cecchi Gori, and the show has been slightly less than objective when dealing with Fiorentina's problems.

On April 6, as the season moved into the final stretch, *Biscardi's Trial* dealt with the 'blitz' visit of Juve star Alessandro Del Piero to London, Massimo Moratti's salvo aimed at Juventus and their supposed control of the refs, Milan's crisis, Edmundo's comeback, and who's a more valuable player – Ronaldo or Pippo Inzaghi of Juventus?

Each one of the subjects was a worthy theme for an intelligent table conversation, but that's not the idea for this show. Biscardi wants a free for all, and gets it. Sometimes five people scream at

---

were published, and a week later *La Gazzetta* asked for another piece on the Brazilian. He went back to the Udinese training camp, but Zico wasn't around. 'So I talked with the players and the Mister and put together all the material that I had previously collected,' Mosca explained. The problem was that the headline writers then topped the piece with a bold LISTEN UP, PLATINI, which made it look like Zico was challenging Juve's French champion. This tends to happen a lot in Italy – quotes in the headlines that are nowhere in the story. That's what Zico didn't like and why he claimed on TV that he hadn't given the interview.

once, and Mosca rarely misses his chance to get red in the face. Some of those in the audience like to get into the action as well, usually by holding up signs of discontent with a team or coach or player.

Biscardi's show did reveal one little scoop. The transmission came just on the heels of the Lazio–Juventus match, played in Rome, which Juve managed to win 1–0. The referee, Pierluigi Collina, was bitterly criticized for not giving a penalty on an alleged hand ball in the closing minutes of the game. As usual, Juve came under assault for favoured treatment on the field.

But Biscardi promised at the beginning of the show that viewers would learn who Collina roots for. One of the guests, Danilo di Tommaso, who writes for *TuttoSport*, had dug out an old article from a now-defunct Naples weekly, *Sport Sud*. Collina, who was then working in Serie D, had spoken with the magazine after refereeing a match between Sarnese and Battipagliese. 'I've always been a *simpatizzante* of Lazio,' the ref responded when asked who he liked in the big leagues. But Lazio fans were not convinced, and continued to blame Collina for making them lose their biggest match of the season.

Television viewers had the chance to call in their votes on two questions that both, wisely, involved Juventus, the country's most popular team. Question one: If you had to choose one player, would you take Del Piero or Ronaldo? Question two: Is Inzaghi worth less as a scorer than Ronaldo or Del Piero? Juve's fans came through for their boys. Sixty per cent of those who called in said they would prefer Del Piero to Ronaldo; another 60 per cent said no, Inzaghi was not worth less as a scorer than either his team-mate Del Piero or Ronaldo.

The show had a live hook-up with Edmundo, who won the 'Pryngeps★ Award' for his goal and assist in Fiorentina's 2–1 victory over Parma the day before. Someone pointed out how Fiorentina bought Batistuta for only 4 billion lire (less than £1.5 million) and Edmundo for 'only' 11 billion (or about £4 million), 'a drop

★ The watch-maker, and sponsor of the show.

138

in the bucket in this world of football'. In other words, great work, Mr Cecchi Gori. You are a genius.

Biscardi hooked up with Edmundo and congratulated him on his performance against Parma. 'You showed right away what kind of champion you are,' he told the Brazilian. Well, not really. As a matter of fact, right away he sat on the bench and then went back pouting to Brazil. But no matter. The new Edmundo was back with a soft voice and a soft demeanour.

'I'm very happy,' the player said in a language somewhere between Italian and Portuguese. 'The people in Florence are beautiful. Now Florence very good. Let's hope we go in UEFA.' Biscardi asked his correspondent in Florence to translate. The correspondent translated quite freely, making up a bunch of stuff about how Edmundo still misses Brazil but that winning makes him miss it less. They ask him how he gets along with Batistuta, Fiorentina's top scorer. 'Batistuta is a beautiful guy, a beautiful person,' Edmundo says. 'I really like Italy a lot.' Yeah. At 60,000 quid a month, it's hard not to.

Biscardi sent his compliments to Cecchi Gori for 'believing' in Edmundo. Actually, they had been fighting for the better part of a couple of months. Someone commented that Edmundo was as good as Ronaldo, which triggered a chorus of boos from the *Interisti* in the studio. Anything to boost your audience.

Biscardi's Trial also discussed the controversial comments of Internazionale's owner Massimo Moratti after Juve's 1–0 victory over Lazio, which kept *La Signora* in 1st place, one point ahead of Moratti's squad. Juve and Inter were scheduled to play at Turin in three weeks' time, the fourth-from-last match of the season. 'We'll go to Turin to win, not to watch the others play,' Moratti said. 'As long as we play eleven against eleven. Allow me at least this nastiness.'

That single phrase, 'as long as we play eleven against eleven', became the subject of a week's worth of debate about Juventus and the referees. The discussion on Biscardi's show was particularly heated. Some excerpts:

Gino Menicucci (a former referee): This is terribly grave if there are these suspicions . . .

Aldo Biscardi: Why is there is war between Inter and Juve twenty days before the game? What's happened?

Italo Cucci: To speak three weeks before the game in order to condition the referee is useless.

Maurizio Mosca: The bad blood between Inter and Juventus is atavistic.

Caterina Collovati: There is this great effort to discredit Juve's season, which has been marvellous.

[Four or five people start talking at the same time.]

Cucci: The referee awarded six minutes of injury time. He wouldn't do that if he wanted to favour Juventus.

The fortune-teller: But he didn't have the courage to assign the penalty shot!

Mosca: Six minutes doesn't make all that much difference.

[Shouting continues as Cucci and Menicucci try to keep up with Mosca.]

Menicucci: Mosca, you listen for once. You always interrupt!

[Mosca stands up in anger.]

Blondie: [smiling] Time for the adverts!

[Tempers calm down during break for ads about cars, whiskey and tyres. This is a man's show. No perfume or skin creams or floor cleaners for sale here. The tension rises again once the show resumes.]

Cucci: [obviously stunned by the six-minute decision] If a referee allows the losing team to play for six minutes of injury time . . . they're not upset about the officiating, but that they didn't manage to win.

Jacobelli: Why do we need this culture of suspicion?

Menicucci: Do we believe in these referees or not? If not, then we have to do something. I think Collina is a decent person.

Biscardi: Nobody denies that.

Menicucci: What do you mean nobody denies that?

Cucci: Don't you think a bad game for [striker Roberto] Mancini costs Lazio a lot more than a bad call?

The fortune-teller: When you lose a game, it's always the fault of the referee.

Irene Pivetti: [very calmly, as she has had a lot of experience with rows at the House of Deputies]: The entire category of referees is in crisis. The refs should be strong figures, a guarantee for weak teams. We have to reinforce their authority.

Cucci: The ref who's been bought – I'm speaking about many years ago – doesn't give himself away on the penalty shot given or not given. He shows himself in the little things at centre field.

Menicucci: If you buy *Gazzetta dello Sport* from ten years ago on Monday, you'll hear all these same arguments.

Truer words were never spoken, and a nice ending to a bitter argument. Biscardi said it was time to move on and talk about Juventus. Xavier Jacobelli of *TuttoSport* had prepared a short presentation of Juve's recent successes, and the winning combination up front of Inzaghi and Del Piero. Jacobelli said Inzaghi could be the Paolo Rossi of France '98. That was a big if, but one that would make Juventus fans happy. Paolo Rossi scored six goals in three games – including three against Brazil – for the Azzuri when Italy won the World Cup in Spain in 1982.

Biscardi moved on to the *moviola*, the replay of controversial decisions in the Lazio–Juventus match. The panellists looked at five different encounters, and argued about every one except the first, a piece of dangerous play by Lazio's Alen Boksic that may have given the home team a goal had the ref let it pass. The others were more controversial: a Lazio defender stepping on Del Piero's foot in the penalty area (no whistle); Del Piero and Nesta colliding as the ball approaches the goal (foul called against Del Piero); Lazio midfielder Pavel Nedved given a yellow card for a foul, and a red card immediately afterwards for telling the ref to go bugger himself.

There was plenty to argue about on the last replay, the Lazio corner kick blocked by the hand of a leaping Juventus defender, Mark Iuliano. While Lazio asked for a penalty shot, Collina determined that it wasn't intentional and let play proceed. Lazio may have lost its chance for a *scudetto* in that brief moment. Their owner, Sergio Cragnotti, would later remark, 'In football, the colour of your jerseys counts a whole lot.'

After hearing the pros and cons of Collina's performance in Lazio–Juve, Biscardi called for silence and Blondie smiled and said it was time for '*telepromotions*'. After the break everyone listened politely to a presentation on Milan's *via crucis*, prepared by Italo Cucci. Fabio Capello's team had lost their third game straight, 1–0 to struggling Bari.

The discussion about Milan immediately got Mosca yelling and red in the face again, apparently angry that in the depth of their crisis, Milan players were unable to dig up some of that former pride. Someone else pointed out that Edgar Davids was emblematic of Milan's problems. Juve's brilliant midfielder had rested his butt on the bench at Milan, but flourished after he changed into zebra stripes four games into the season.

Pivetti, a *Milanista* who's much more at home on political talk-shows, offered this: everybody's tired at the end of the season, and they don't handle the tension well. Pivetti's husband, who also goes on Biscardi's show, expressed his disappointment that veteran players such as Paolo Maldini and Alessandro Costacurta haven't seemed to react to the crisis.

Menicucci said Milan coach Fabio Capello was right to get angry and say he's ashamed of the squad. Soon four people were talking at once, and Mosca, of course, was not one of those sitting on the sidelines. Biscardi calmed them down and said get ready, because in a few short minutes the fortune-teller was going to tell us who would win the *scudetto*. Blondie smiled and said it was time for adverts. This time we heard from Nintendo, Campari and Nike.

The fortune-teller predicted Inter would win the *scudetto* this season (Juve fans were not pleased). He also said Del Piero would

142

be the *capocannoniere*, or top scorer, which made the *Juventini* happy. The fortune-teller turned out to be wrong on both counts. He claimed Lazio would win the UEFA Cup and the Italian Cup. That pleased Lazio fans, but in fact the Eagles only won the Italian Cup.

Mosca also had a prediction, which he managed to make in a nearly normal tone of voice: that Inter would give striker Youri Djorkaeff and 20 billion lire to Barcelona in exchange for midfielder Ivan de la Pena. Biscardi said goodbye, Blondie smiled, and two hours of shouting came to an end. They may be rude and loud, but Biscardi's guests are successful at bringing bar-stool arguments on to television. Nobody looks drunk, but given the tone of the arguments, they certainly could be. The show has an average of more than a million viewers each week.

Paolo Brosio was at the wheel of the Bluesmobile, and Blues Brother Dan Ackroyd sat in the passenger seat as they cruised the streets of Rome on a Sunday afternoon late in the season. There was a Catholic nun, Suor Paola, in the back seat. She seemed slightly amused. Brosio, a special correspondent for the football programme *Quelli Che il Calcio*, might have the best job in Italy. He gets paid to do any number of outrageous things on Sunday afternoon to keep football fans entertained.

Sometimes his escapades actually have something to do with football. He'll go to Munich to spend the afternoon with an Italian playing at Bayern, Ruggiero Rizzitelli, for example. But often his little jaunts are simply tricks to keep the fans entertained while their favourite teams fight it out on the field. He may go for a long bike ride on the day the Giro d'Italia starts, or do New York, passing the afternoon at the Fashion Café in the company of top model Eva Herzigova. Tough job, indeed. He once played fetch-it boy for Elton John when the singer visited the Milan studio of the show.

Quelli Che manages to bring in a fair number of surprising guests, and on one Sunday used a former government minister, Piero Barucci, as their reporter at a Fiorentina–Sampdoria game. Barucci got awfully excited when Fiorentina took the lead with Gabriel

Batistuta's 100th goal in Serie A, and tried to celebrate by making '100' signs with his fingers. He needed the help of his sidekick, a singer named Pupo, for the second zero. It was pretty absurd, but made for good TV. Somehow it's hard to imagine Robin Cook or Madeline Albright screaming into the microphone on national TV: 'Take that, man; 100 goals for the big guy!' In the end Barucci's excitement waned a bit. Sampdoria equalized, and the game ended 1–1.

Brosio once entertained his fans from an apartment in Bologna by waiting for a couple of actresses to show up. One of the women, Nancy Brilli, is quite popular, and Brosio hooked up a fax machine in the window of the flat so Nancy's admirers could send her messages. Brosio, who was being filmed from the square below, could then relay the messages to the show. The faxes came rolling in – Brilli is a very attractive woman – but the best one was for Brosio. He may be in his late 30s and balding, but has a great personality. Really very simpatico. A young woman admirer faxed him a note in huge letters that said, 'Brosio, I'll marry you by July.' He got a big kick out of that, and told the audience how happy it would make his mother, who's worried that her boy needs to settle down.

Quelli Che il Calcio is essentially souped-up radio. Since the matches can't be transmitted on public television, Italian men have spent Sunday afternoons attached to their radios for years. *Quelli Che* gives the same information – and a lot more, if you like Brosio – in televised form. There are updates on every goal, and reports from various grounds. A reporter might be sent to Parma, for example, to watch the game with Gigi Buffon's mother, Stella. She's quite at home on camera, and has become a regular correspondent. In the studio there are supporters from each team, including the now-famous Idris, a Senegalese who follows Juventus. Idris was unknown until *Quelli Che* made him practically a household name in Italy.

It's a good mix of serious journalists, the occasional fortune-teller, humorous *tifosi* such as the actor Leo Teocoli, of Milan, and the nun, Suor Paola. Teocoli does a great imitation of Milan's general director, Adriano Galliano. During Milan's terrible year, Teocoli found it easy to mimic Galliano's facial movements as he watched the matches: frown, frown and frown some more.

Of course, since it's Italian, on television, and produced for a mostly male audience, the show wouldn't be complete without a few babes, would-be starlets, models and the like. The programme has been running for five years, and has an audience of more than 4 million each Sunday. It's not easy to keep people entertained for two hours straight, and *Quelli Che* has high moments and low, but Brosio scores every Sunday.

15 Pinko Papers and Fantasy Calcio

La Gazzetta dello Sport doesn't look much like a man's newspaper. It's printed on pink paper, after all. But *La Gazzetta* leads the pack of Italy's sports dailies, selling more than 600,000 copies a day, almost all of them to men and boys. The adverts are mostly for cars, tyres, motor oil and sports television.

While it's technically a sports newspaper, the main sport in the country is *calcio*, and that's what *La Gazzetta* covers passionately. The paper, which recently celebrated its 100th anniversary, also finds space for Formula One, cycling, skiing, and occasionally sailing. But during the season, Serie A takes up the first half of the paper, which also gives a few pages to Serie B.

La Gazzetta is published by Rizzoli in Milan, in the same building as *Corriere della Sera*, and tends to favour coverage of the strong northern squads over the Rome teams. Even though Lazio spent much of the second half of the season in the running for the *scudetto*, you would have never known it reading the front page of the pink paper. INTER–JUVE DUEL or INTER BITES JUVE were typical headlines during the year. After only the seventh game of the 34-game season, when Inter beat Parma (then in 3rd place) and Juventus topped Udinese, the *Gazzetta* announced: 'Already It's Inter–Juve.' Lazio would later come along with 16 games without a loss to make it a three-way race, and the paper would be forced to pay attention to the *biancocelesti*, or blue and whites, but not until they pulled within two points of 1st-place Juventus.

La Gazzetta has the lion's share of Italy's football fans, but faces competition in Rome from *Corriere dello Sport*, with a circulation of 350,000, and in Turin from *TuttoSport*, which sells about 90,000 a day. *Corriere dello Sport* recently bought *TuttoSport*, although they continue to publish two separate papers.

The papers are hardly coy about their favourites in Serie A. While Gazzetta favours the Milan teams, *Corriere dello Sport* has the two squads in the capital, and *TuttoSport* the teams from Turin. While everyone knows about Juve, the city also hosts Torino, which had a glorious past but slipped into Serie B after the 1995–96 season.

When Massimo Moratti of Inter quipped in early April that his squad would go to Torino later in the month to beat Juventus 'as long as we play eleven against eleven', *La Gazzetta* placed it on the front page but didn't overplay it. A front-page commentary about the season, and especially the battle between Inter and Juventus, didn't even mention it until the very end of the article, calling Moratti's words 'inopportune'.

But the Rome paper, *Corriere dello Sport*, was still stinging from Saturday night's 0–1 Lazio–Juventus result, and revelled in the subtle accusation of referees favouring Agnelli's team. MORATTI TO JUVE: LET'S PLAY CLEAN blared the headline, and inside there was a full page dedicated to how Juventus allegedly stole the game from Lazio. The newspaper interviewed seventy players to ask if, in their opinion, there should have been a hand foul called against Juventus in the penalty area (55 said yes; 15 no). Lazio striker Roberto Mancini was quoted saying that next year the team should wear black and white jerseys (like Juve's) instead of blue and white. Lazio fans were angry, and Moratti's teasing Juventus added more fuel to their fire.

TuttoSport was stuck in its own little world of Turin, one of Italy's more depressing industrial cities, and the top headline celebrated Juve striker Pippo Inzaghi's performance from three days before: INZAGHI: 100 OF THESE GOALS. They followed that with MORATTI ATTACKS LA JUVE, and dedicated a front-page editorial to the subject, as if *La Signora* had willingly lost her innocence.

The commentary, by Darwin Pastorin, ran under the headline ABSURD SUSPICIONS. 'The words of football are heavy, and unbearable,' he began. 'The truth is that power wears out those who don't have it. And Juventus, first place in the table and already a Champions League Finalist, bothers the others and makes them envious.'

Pastorin mentioned not only Moratti's comments about eleven against eleven, but also his claim that Inter have never had the 'historical power' of Juventus. The writer also repeated the angry words of Lazio president Sergio Cragnotti ('the colour of the jerseys was decisive'), which cost Cragnotti a £1700 fine from the league.

'All this story about Juve which is protected by the referees, about Juve that wins because it's a financial superpower, has become tiresome,' Pastorin wrote. 'We have great esteem for Cragnotti and Moratti. Why do they have to stoop to these levels?'

Pastorin didn't mention that Juve's defenders on the last corner kick looked more like they were playing volleyball than football; he made no reference whatsoever to the questionable call. As for financial power, nobody wins in Serie A any more without deep pockets; the only question is how deep.

Pastorin neglected to mention the game Juventus had just won, knocking Lazio out of the running for the *scudetto*. Instead, he solemnly declared that football could do without a climate of suspicion. 'Football, and above all its enlightened directors, should remain calm and respect those who, day after day, with work, with deeds, with goals, have built up worldwide credibility,' he pontificated. 'And season after season, despite the sale of star players, continue to win. Against everything and everybody.'

Amen, brother. And don't forget to praise Juventus. That's not to say *TuttoSport* is the only paper that plays partisan football. *La Gazzetta dello Sport*, and its editor, Candido Cannavo, launched a campaign to bring Roberto Baggio to the World Cup that didn't let up until May 21, when the manager of the national team, Cesare Maldini, finally brought the *fantasista* into the fold. Baggio was ecstatic; Gianfranco Zola, who was left at home, a little less so. Zola complained that he didn't have the 'sponsorship' some others enjoyed.

But there were some problems with Roby. Although he is a clear sentimental favourite, not only in Italy but also worldwide, he's an ageing striker who sat on the bench at Milan and can divide a team – and the nation – if he doesn't get to play. Ancelotti feared that leaving him on the bench could create problems inside the dressing room.

And for all of his wizardry, Baggio is best known for having missed his penalty in the Italy–Brazil World Cup Final in 1994 in Los Angeles. That was when Fiat chief Gianni Agnelli, for whom Baggio once played at Juventus, named him the 'wet rabbit'. Agnelli doesn't need many words to make himself clear.

It's the ultimate sport for a wannabe footballer who's not big enough or fast enough or tough enough. *Fantacalcio*, or Fantasy Football, is played by millions of Italians, and there's not a barracks or a classroom in Italy that doesn't have its own imaginary championship. *La Gazzetta dello Sport* alone has more than 200,000 people who compete in its competition. The pink paper's prize winner walks away with a very cool BMW coupé, the Z3.

While it sounds just like a game a newspaper might make up to boost sales, it's an entire fantasy world. There's a Fantasy Football Federation and you can win Fantasy Cups or the Super Fantasy Champions Cup. *La Gazzetta* lists the top 10 Fantasy Coaches of each week, and the Fantasy Coach of the Year drives off in the BMW.

Football fanatics love this game, and lose hours and hours poring over statistics as they try to put together the winning combinations. Players have 270 'fantasy billion lire' to buy a squad: three keepers, eight defenders, eight midfielders, and six strikers. There's no limit on non-European players.

Once you've put together your team you call a special number at *La Gazzetta* and punch in the codes for your players (cost of the call is more than 1000 lire a minute). Each week you can change your starting formation, and also buy and sell players. And your points are calculated on the mark that *Gazzetta* gives the player in question for his game that week (normally a number

149

between 5 and 8). (To that, other numbers are added, i.e., 3 points for a goal, 3 points for a penalty shot stopped by your keeper. You can also lose points: 1 for every goal taken, 3 for every penalty shot missed, ½ for every yellow card.)

At the end of the season the better players have racked up more than 2500 points, and perhaps a hundred pounds in phone bills as well. And, of course, they've bought *La Gazzetta* faithfully every day. Most of all, they've had fun, making up team names like All Potatoes, Top Gun, Ciao Mamma, The Buffaloes Broke Out of the Pen, and Bulgarians Try Again.

Boys just want to have fun. And they are almost all boys, although it was a woman 'manager' who was leading the pack for most of the '97–98 season in *La Gazzetta*'s competition. But in the end it was actually a two-man management team that drove away with the prize. Milan students Emanuele Robbioni's and Alessandro Bonetti's squad, 'We Wanted Ronaldo But . . .' overtook Alessandra Cerioni's 'Ancona Team' in the final match of the season and won the *fanta-scudetto*. How do you divide a BMW convertible? That wasn't as difficult as it seemed. Robbioni doesn't have a driver's licence, and was planning to sell his share to Bonetti.

16 A Boy from Brazil

Even if his football career were to end tomorrow, 21-year-old Luis Nazario Ronaldo, better known by those last three syllables, or as the Phenomenon, could dwell for quite some time about the glories of the past. The 1994 World Cup Championship with Brazil, for example. Or an astounding 55 goals in 56 games with PSV Eindhoven, and 47 goals in 49 games with Barcelona. Then there's the FIFA Player of the Year award (twice), and the Golden Ball award. But there's one award he hasn't yet nailed down, and that's the *scudetto*.

He was not far away from that goal for most of the season, since his squad, Internazionale, led for the first half of the year, and spent most of the return leg only a point behind league-leaders Juventus. But Ronaldo was the first to point out that Serie A is serious stuff. 'It's the best league in the world, and certainly the most difficult,' the Phenom says. 'Winning the championship in Italy is more difficult than winning the World Cup.'

Italy is the Broadway of world football, and was the logical next stop for Ronaldo (and his sponsor, Nike) after stints in the Netherlands and Spain. The Serie A squads began a bidding war for the young Brazilian after he scored nearly a goal a game for Barcelona. Inter eventually won that battle. Oilman Massimo Moratti's squad were hungry for a *scudetto*, which they had not won since the 1988–89 season.

Inter sponsor Pirelli, which has extensive holdings in Brazil, was also happy to have the striker. After the runners Carl Lewis and Marie-Jo Perec, Pirelli has turned to Ronaldo in their 'Power Without Control is Nothing' advertising campaign. In a print ad that has sparked some criticism from Catholic circles, Ronaldo is pictured from behind, perched above Rio de Janiero with his arms outstretched in the same way as the Christ the Redeemer statue at Corcovado. The Archbishop of Rio de Janeiro, Eugenio de Sales, took offence at the ad, as did the Italian Cardinal Ersilio Tonini, who called it a 'lack of taste and very indecent'. Other figures in the Catholic hierarchy also jumped in to denounce Pirelli's campaign. But Don Mazzi, a priest who appears frequently on TV — and an Inter supporter — said he wasn't shocked in the least. 'All I see in it is a sportsman who chooses a statue as a symbol of his city,' Mazzi said. Ronnie didn't consider the image blasphemous, either. 'I'm Catholic; I believe in God, and the image is beautiful,' said the number 10. 'Besides, I'm pictured in the same position I take when I score a goal: arms outstretched, index fingers extended. I've never played on a top team in Rio, and this is a way of being close to my city.'

He's got power and he's got control, but could Ronaldo be Inter's saviour? He came pretty close. After 29 league games he had scored 21 goals, tied for the top scorer's spot with Oliver Bierhoff of Udinese, and was ahead of Juve's Alessandro Del Piero. Ronaldo also electrified crowds whenever he played. Season-ticket sales for Inter jumped from 35,000 to 48,000, and the team has brought in an average of 65,000 fans for each game, a record for Serie A this season.

Inter didn't win the *scudetto*, and yet, Ronaldo made the difference for them. During his goal drought in January he scored just 1 goal in 7 games. But in the following two months, he scored 14 goals in 14 games, bringing Inter to the final of the UEFA Cup and keeping them on Juve's heels. Ronaldo may not have managed to score a goal a game in Serie A, but no foreigner playing for his first year in the Italian championship has ever matched Ronaldo's 25 goals. The great Platini tallied only 14 at Juventus in 1982–83, the same as Maradona at Napoli in 1984–85.

'Ronaldo is probably the first planetary icon that football has produced,' says Lanfranco Vaccari of the Milan-based *La Gazzetta dello Sport*. 'It wasn't Pelé because the world wasn't connected like it is now. And it wasn't Maradona because he was *maux dit*.

152

Ronaldo's young, simpatico, and does things that no one has done before him. He's not the best player in the history of football, but there's never been a centre-forward who's so strong and and skilful at handling the ball on the run. I don't think there's ever been a centre-forward who could run 50 metres as fast as he does, and he does it with the ball attached to his feet.'

Ronaldo is the Michael Jordan of football, and has the advantage of playing a sport that is better known worldwide. True, he can't score 63 goals a game, but even if he only scores one, or provides a brilliant assist that sets up the winner, as he did for French team-mate Youri Djorkaeff in Inter's 1–0 victory over Juventus on January 4, that's enough. At Inter's home stadium, San Siro, it is enough for Ronaldo to touch the ball, and the crowd, frequently 80,000 strong, begins to roar.

The global crowd also makes noise. When Ronaldo agreed to go on-line for the United Nations Food and Agriculture Organization, some six million people tried making computer contact with the new Pelé. Ronaldomania, which only increased with the start of the World Cup, has a particularly interesting manifestation among young Inter fans. Thousands of kids in Milan have shaved their scalps in imitation of football's rising star; at least in the barbershop they can do what they can't manage to accomplish on the field. Their mothers, however, are generally not impressed.

When he takes off his black and blue-striped Pirelli shirt and Nike shoes and comes home from work (usually driving a silver Ferrari that was a gift from his three agents) Ronaldo is a laid-back young man who likes to sleep. He also hangs out with his companion Susana Werner, a Brazilian he may or may not marry. A Brazilian newspaper reported that he and Susana, also called 'Ronaldinha', would tie the knot after the World Cup. But Ronaldo insists that this is 'his business' and that he's never said when he'd be getting married.

Ronaldo is what the Italians call a *bravo ragazzo*, a nice boy. But the 'nice boy' has a number of tough protectors; if Bill Clinton had such handlers he would have never gotten in trouble. Ronaldo virtually stopped talking to the Italian press during his mid-season slump, when journalists attributed his poor performance to late nights in Milan discos. And yet, it's hard to imagine Ronnie as a party animal. He's softspoken and even shy. The animal in him comes out only on the pitch.

Although Inter spent much of the season not talking to the media, what they call *silenzio stampa*, the pressure for Ronaldo was so great before the World Cup that occasionally Inter's press office would organize small encounters with foreign journalists to meet the Phenomenon. But, ultimately, it's a little disappointing. You arrive at Appiano Gentile, Inter's training ground near Lake Como, with the same kind of tension that hits when you've got an appointment with a pope or a prime minister. The tape recorder has been tested three times, and you're determined not to lose a single word of this brief encounter.

But then, what happens? How does it all fall apart? The words are, well, those of a 21-year-old kid in a blue training suit and plastic Nike sandals, who really doesn't want to say too much. He talks but he doesn't really converse. He's polite and smiles, and gently kids a woman from Inter's media affairs office about her smoking. He doesn't like it. Maybe that's the way to stop Ronaldo, to blow smoke in his face. He responds to questions, but usually without excessive detail.

GB: Who's your barber?
R: [rubbing his skull] I do it myself.
GB: How often?
R: I don't know, whenever it needs it.
GB: Do you do it yourself to save money?
R: No, you know. It's just easier, you buy the razor and that's that.
GB: What do you think now that Barcelona has won the Spanish championship?
R: I'm very happy for my former team.
GB: You've said the Italian championship is more difficult than the Spanish one. What do you find most difficult? The strong defence? The press?

R: I don't like lies, which is what are written here. There are a lot of lies in the paper. This is why we've gone into press silence. It's a difficult league, but we have a strong team.

GB: How would you defend against Ronaldo if you were coach of the opposite team?

R: [smiles] I don't know. It's like when we played against Juventus or Milan. You've got to be careful on every play, every action. And don't let him go.

GB: What are Brazil's chances in the World Cup?

R: Brazil will be very strong, but we need some time to get better. Brazil has always had teams that were strong on attack, but now it looks like we have a better defence, as well.

GB: You've said your greatest joy is scoring a goal. But now you're going to get married. Isn't that maybe bigger?

R: [smiling but determined to set the record straight] I never said when I'm getting married. That's my business. But scoring goals is beautiful, exalting.

GB: What were your first memories as a child about the World Cup?

R: I always heard about the World Cup as the most beautiful competition in football, and the most important. I used to dream about playing in it.

GB: But you didn't get any playing time in the US in 1994.

R: No, but it was very useful all the same.

GB: How do you feel about representing your country, which is so football crazy?

R: It's a great responsibility for us players, and we know we have to do well, since there are so many people rooting for us. I'm sure we'll do the best we can.

GB: You once told a journalist that you don't like being called the Phenomenon. Is that true?

R: No, it's not that I don't like the nickname. I like it, but I'm not a phenomenon. I try to do my best, play well, at my top level. I'm happy with what I'm doing.

155

GB: With all the great football players out there, why is it that you've become the icon?

R: Huhh? [Then, after a little re-phrasing of the question] Maybe because I played for a year in Spain, where the press is very strong, and scored a lot of goals. That may have helped. And then I came to Italy, which is the most difficult championship in the world, and scored a lot of goals here, too.

GB: You've already become a kind of legend at 21. How do you deal with that?

R: It's not important for me to become a legend or an idol. I just want to do well now. What I want to do now is play well, then afterwards enjoy life. Because playing, one suffers. A ten-year career is very tough. You suffer because you can't be home with your family and you're always with the team. I like it, but it could be better. Like they do in the United States with basketball. They play a lot of games but then they get three or four months off. All we get is three or four weeks. We have a lot of important competitions on our calendar.

GB: Do you follow any other sports?

R: Basketball.

GB: Anyone in particular you like?

R: Jordan.

GB: Does the fact you get paid so much cause any problems for you, psychologically?

R: That I'm paid so much? Certainly not a problem. I work hard and I do my best to earn my salary. I think it's right that they pay me for what I do.

GB: But doesn't all the attention cause problems for you?

R: I try to do the best I can, to do my work well. The attention comes from you guys, the journalists.

GB: Did you always want to be famous?

R: Yeah, even when I was little, I wanted to be the best. I wanted to play well. I wanted to be famous, but this is not important. I wanted to be the best, not just one among many.

GB: Do you follow your home page on the Internet?

R: Yeah, I get a lot of nasty mail. I haven't answered it yet, but I will.

GB: What kind of nasty mail?

R: Like after we lost 5–0 to Milan [in the Italian Cup] a bunch of people wrote in and said, 'You're S—!'

Ronaldo didn't even want to use the S-word. Either he's too much of a gentleman, the proverbial nice boy, or he's been trained extremely well by his handlers. Inter's manager, Gigi Simoni, takes it a step up from a *bravo ragazzo*. For Simoni, the Phenomenon's not only nice, he's a 'wonderful boy'. In addition, Simoni suggests, and this is a slightly more important for Inter's purposes, Ronnie's the greatest player in the world. 'But he's only at about 60 per cent of his potential,' Simoni offers, triggering wild dreams of what Ronaldo would look like at 100 per cent if what we're getting is only a little more than half. You want to yell out, 'Hey, Ronnie, wake up! Quit holding back on us!'

It seems like a joke, but Simoni is serious. 'Because he's still young, he still has a lot to learn, and needs a lot more experience,' the Mister says. Simoni believes Ronaldo lacks some equilibrium. 'At this point, he still needs to rest, to recover from time to time. When he finds his balance he'll be better as a player.' Simoni says his star attacker has natural physical talent, and technically isn't missing much either. He's also a smart player, but could make some improvement here, the Mister muses. 'He's very intuitive and lively,' says Simoni, pointing out what Italy's best defenders have learned the hard way. 'He's got a good head on his shoulders, but it's not used at its best right now because right now he's the best player in the world and it's very easy for him. But I think he could become the best player of all time.'

An exaggeration? Perhaps, or perhaps not. The man who brought him to Milan, Massimo Moratti, has run out of descriptions for the Phenomenon. 'You find the adjectives,' shrugs Moratti. 'I don't have any left.'

★   ★   ★

Even the greatest player in the world makes mistakes, as Parma learned with pleasant surprise on March 8, the 24th game of the regular season in Serie A. Ronaldo isn't supposed to have any defects. Perhaps his new boots failed him in the crucial moment. No matter. Parma–Inter was 0–0 when defender Zé Maria was called for a foul on Ronaldo in the area. A questionable call, but the Brazilian went to take the shot, which would presumably put Inter in the lead, earn them three points and keep them close to 1st-place Juventus.

After months of research, Nike had come out with a new shoe, the Mercurial, which Ronaldo was wearing for the first time in a real game. Nike had used a midfielder from a mid-table Serie C team, Brescello, to test the new shoes for nearly a year before they were placed on Ronnie's fabled feet. Corrado Oldoni, a former factory worker, resembles Ronaldo not so much in his ability but in the size and shape of his feet, which are quite small, only 41½. Oldoni wrote six different reports for Nike about the performance of the Mercurial so the company could perfect the product.

The Phenomenon put his head down, aimed and fired, but it was the wrong day for Nike's debut. You won't be seeing that shot in any of their adverts, since Parma's keeper, Gigi Buffon, has a contract with Fila. Buffon guessed right by diving left, and blocked the shot, which was hard and low. It wasn't a bad kick, but Buffon proved why he's one of the keepers on the Italian national team, even though he's only 20. Defender Lilian Thuram used his Nikes (not Mercurials) to clear the rebound and Parma held Inter scoreless. Mercury, the messenger of the gods, failed to deliver the goals on this particular Sunday.

Parma striker Hernán Crespo found himself with the ball in front of the goal when Inter failed to cover him on a corner kick, and Ancelotti's squad notched up a 1–0 victory. Crespo's old-fashioned Nikes worked just fine for him. 'I'm going to stay with these ones,' the Argentine joked after the game. When Nike released the Mercurial they promised that the new product offered stability, traction and comfort. 'The ultra-light boots are made for players for whom speed and control are everything,' the company said. 'With Nike Mercurial on your feet the situation is always under control.' Maybe they better make that 'almost always.' They didn't work wonders for Brescello's Oldoni, either, who had scored only one goal for the season by the time Ronaldo started using his boots.

17 Blame the Ref (You Might be Right)

Lazio fans talked for weeks about how they had been robbed of any chance for the *scudetto* by Pierluigi Collina's failure to award a penalty for hand ball in the closing minutes of the Lazio–Juventus fixture. Juve won 0–1. One rabid Lazio fan, Daniela Fini, went so far as to say Lazio would have been at the top were it not for errors on the part of the *arbitri* that hurt the team.

Daniela is not just any fan. As wife of Gianfranco Fini, the party secretary of the National Alliance (heirs to the Italian fascists), Daniela is one of the better known *Laziali* (along with the nun, Suor Paola), and journalists are constantly asking her opinion about the games. She didn't mince words about the 0–1 Lazio–Juventus result. 'I'd like to pose a question to the gentlemen running Italian football,' she said. 'Why do we continue with this farce of a championship and *scudetto* if we know from the very beginning that Juventus have got to win it? It's all written, it's all programmed, just like a script.'

Mrs Fini complimented Juve for their ability, and was especially impressed by strikers Alessandro Del Piero and Filippo Inzaghi, and midfielder Edgar Davids, but said the referees have a 'complex' regarding Juventus that doesn't allow them to look at a match fairly. 'Let's look at Collina for now,' Mrs Fini said. 'Because the penalty shot he failed to give in injury time wasn't the only pearl of that match. What about the offsides on Boksic when Nedved was going to the goal alone? And Nedved's getting booked for cursing? Does Collina know how many vulgarities are uttered on the pitch? It's natural, you're playing a match that's worth the entire season.'

Some people have suggested that foreign refs be brought in

160

for important matches, but Daniela Fini doesn't agree. She wants Italians. But only if they're subject to the same sanctions as the players. That they be given warnings, that they have to miss a match, or that they be banned altogether from the game. 'If you make a mistake, you should pay the price,' she said.

It was ironic that one of the most controversial games of the season took place under the watchful eye of Pierluigi Collina, who was voted best ref by the players. He ran the Olympic Final match in Atlanta and was also called for the World Cup. Like in Britain, the referees are known by towns from which they come, and Collina is listed in the papers as 'Collina of Viareggio'. But he is most easily recognized on account of his spectral appearance, and there are few football fans who don't know his name. Several years ago Collina suffered alopecia, which left him completely bald, and he appears much older than his 38 years.

Lazio–Juve wasn't the only match in which the *arbitro* proved decisive to the outcome, and Lazio often ended up with the short end of the stick. In Lazio–Inter at the beginning of the season, Inter, who had been losing, were able to salvage a 1–1 draw thanks to a penalty kick given for a highly dubious foul. The ref also erroneously awarded a penalty shot to Juventus in a Lazio–Juventus match in December, allowing the black and whites to win, 2–1.

But it isn't always the big three who benefit. In December, Parma got off lucky twice thanks to the refs. In Florence, they finished 1–1 even though they played more than half the game with ten men, and certainly committed one (if not two) fouls in the penalty area, as Fiorentina assaulted the goal. They were also able to finish 1–1 with Lazio thanks to the award of a questionable penalty.

The criticism of the referees finally became so intense (several different owners were sanctioned by the 'sports judge')★ that they considered going on strike. In the end they simply started all the games 15 minutes late in a sign of protest. The *arbitri* thought they

★ A sports judge is a magistrate named by the Italian football federation.

had put up with enough abuse already, but in fact it had only just begun.

In February, a Napoli defender stopped a shot by Pierluigi Casiraghi with both hands, but no whistle blew and the game ended 0–0. In the same month, in a game that would have Roma fans talking (and yelling) for weeks, no whistle blew when Juve's Didier Deschamps chopped down Roma's Carmine Gautieri. At that point Juve were winning 2–1; a successful penalty shot would have made it 2–2. Instead it ended 3–1 to Juventus.

'There are teams that are privileged, and we aren't among them,' Roma manager Zdenek Zeman declared, calmly. 'And anyone who says the contrary lies and knows that he's lying. Juventus will win the *scudetto*. They have great players and they have advantages that other teams don't have.'

Juve fans often write off the complaints to jealousy. When Lazio's Roberto Mancini made his jibe about Lazio changing from sky-blue jerseys to black and white if they wanted to win, Juventus general director Luciano Moggi responded angrily that Mancini should talk less and play more. Others joked about Juve's alleged favourable treatment. 'Of course they take care of us,' said Andrea Fontana, an economics student. 'If you pay them, that's what they're supposed to do.'

Television executive Clemente Mimun, a *tifoso* of Lazio, pointed to a number of episodes that showed 'disparity of treatment' among the teams in Serie A. 'The black jerseys suffer from an old psychological subjection regarding Juventus,' Mimun said. He called for foreigners to officiate the important matches, whether they be games that decide the *scudetto* or relegation to Serie B: 'They might not be better than our refs, and there will still be polemics, but there would be a lot less suspicion.'

Are Juventus always favoured, or are they just a stronger team and bound to win anyway? This is mostly a recent phenomenon, but there were also polemics back in the eighties, especially in '82 when Juventus just slipped by Roma to win the *scudetto*. The tables were turned a bit, though, when they lost the Champions League Final in 1997 to Borussia Dortmund, and thought they should have had a penalty shot awarded in the opening minutes of the game. Football's talking heads went on for days about how Italy was 'weak' in the international bodies (i.e., they didn't have any sway in appointing favourable refs).

That may or may not be true. What's clear is that a goal changes the nature of the game, and Italian teams – perhaps Juve best of all – know how to hold on to a lead. If Juventus had scored first, the Champions League Final may still have ended 3–1, but Borussia would not have been the squad on top.

Italian referees are currently assigned games by a 'designator', one Fabio Baldas. He gives the bigger matches to the best refs, which is why Collina ran the show for Lazio–Juventus. This system has come under attack, and some owners and managers have called for a random lottery, so that anyone can go anywhere on a given Sunday.

Some, of course, want to see foreigners called in for the big matches. Others, apparently thinking that four eyes are better than two, want to see a second referee brought into the match. Still others think the instant replay, or *moviola*, would solve the problem – something like the National Football League in the US used to have, where everybody got a drink of water while the officials checked out the videotape to tell us what really happened.

Gianni Mura, who comments on *calcio* for *La Repubblica*, has suggested something simple but not revolutionary: let the refs talk. 'Just like a striker or a coach, a ref could decide at the end of the game if he wants to speak – or not – with the journalists and explain why he made some decisions.' Mura noted that the federation has blocked both the officials and their designator from speaking. 'What are they afraid of?' he asked. 'Everybody in football speaks, and a lot of times they shout. The silence of the referees isn't a defence but a handicap, and especially if it's imposed from above.'

After the Juve–Roma match in which the ref, Domenico Messina (of Bergamo), came up short of breath when it was time to blow the whistle against Juventus, Mura still gave him a 6 for his day's work. He was flooded with calls and faxes from Roma

163

fans, who called him a 'northern pig' and asked him how much money he was getting from the Agnelli family, Juve's owners.

Mura, who took all the faxes and put them together with the ones that accuse him of being 'viscerally anti-Juve', said he gave the ref a 6 out of solidarity. 'There are a lot of people who live by replays and freeze frames,' he said. 'But on the field it's different. It was a clear foul of Deschamps on Gautieri. Until then Messina was worthy of an 8. So I took two points away on account of the penalty shot not given, and because for five minutes after that he was completely out of it.'

Even if they got blasted by players, coaches and fans during the season, the refs did find some reason to smile. They got a pay rise. And those who officiate international matches, such as Collina, make about 100 million lire a year (£35000), before taxes. Not bad for a few days' work, but it takes a special breed in Serie A, and one with very thick skin.

On April 19, just two weeks after Collina's most difficult game of the year, the boys from Turin got yet another break, this time courtesy of a ref named Pasquale Rodomonti (of Teramo). It was a crucial week for Juventus, the fifth-last match of the year, and they went to Empoli with just a one-point lead over Inter, who were playing at home against Udinese.

There was no room for error on Juve's part. A tie or a loss would mean Ronaldo and company could take over the league leadership with a victory. Inter won 2−0 and picked up their three points. Juventus, well, they also won, but for the second time in three weeks they probably should have drawn.

Empoli may have been struggling to avoid relegation to Serie B, but, as Parma saw, they were capable of giving a hard time to the better teams, especially at home. They run well, and and can surprise the big guns on occasion. They embarrassed Parma 2−0 in the return leg, and would have probably drawn with Juve were it not for the ref.

After a scoreless first half, Juventus got on the board 24 minutes into the second half when Marcelo Zalayeta found Fabio Pecchia, who beat the Empoli keeper from short range. Seven minutes later, Empoli appeared to have equalized with a header by Stefano Bianconi, but Juve's keeper, Angelo Peruzzi, scooped the ball out of the net, and Rodomonti claimed it hadn't entered.

Of course, the *moviola*, the slow-motion replays, would show otherwise. The entire ball had cleared the line by some 10 centimetres. So instead of going back to Turin with a single point, the *Juventini* went back with three, and were still slightly ahead of Inter and in command of 1st place going into the decisive Juventus—Inter match the following week.

What happened to Mr Rodomonti, who was only three metres away when the ball crossed the line? No one knows, and he wasn't talking. In the heat of the moment he indicated that he had seen the action and that it wasn't a goal. That was that.

Italians love conspiracy theories, *dietrologia*, the study of what's '*dietro*', or behind. And what may have been behind Rodomonti's reluctance to signal a goal for Empoli was something that had happened more than three years earlier. On December 18 1994, Rodomonti had officiated a match between Genoa and Juventus, and mistakenly awarded Genoa a goal that was in reality non-existent. In that case, the ball clearly had not completely crossed the line, just the opposite of what happened at Empoli. But that time the damage was done to Juventus, so perhaps Rodomonti wanted to make up for that sin – or so the anti-Juve psychologists and conspiracy theorists thought, in any case.

What was clear was that he had made a mistake, and Juve had won. All the papers gave the ref a lowly 4 for his work, and that split-second decision did more to harm his future than all the games he had worked up until then. Even the Turin-based *TuttoSport* had to admit that Rodomonti blew it on this one. RODOMONTI RUINS JUVE'S PARTY was the headline over the story.

Juventus were either the best or the most fortunate team in Italian football. Earlier in the season, with another opponent and another ref, exactly the same thing had happened. Udinese's Oliver Bierhoff looked like he had a sure goal, but a sliding Juve defender, Ciro Ferrara, scooped the ball out with his foot (even though it had entered the net completely), and the ref called no goal. Bier-hoff's kick would have given Udinese a 2—1 lead in the game, and put Juve in a difficult position. But that was not apparently in the stars. Juve went on to record a 4—1 victory, and picked up another three points.

The goal denied to Empoli triggered more calls for a 'goal-linesman' who could make that difficult decision, whether or not a ball completely crossed the line. The job would be something similar to the one in tennis, the guy with his finger on top of the net.

Rodomonti came under attack, as did the designator for assigning him to such an important game after his difficult past with Juventus. (Rodomonti had purposefully been kept away from Juventus for three years after the incident with Genoa.)

At the end of the season, Rodomonti confessed that the episode at Empoli was terribly difficult for him after all the insults and criticism he received. 'Even at home life was more difficult,' the ref revealed. 'My wife supports Inter, and she was angry too.' Rodomonti remained bitter about his mistake: 'On account of one episode you risk your entire career, a life of sacrifice . . . so many nice matches that you ran well but that no one remembers.'

The errors made by the refs at Lazio—Juventus and Empoli—Juventus were already enough to have sullied the championship, but when Juve got away with a 1—0 victory against Inter on April 26, it became clear that their *scudetto* for the 1997—98 season was going to need some explaining. Juve's 25th Serie A title would stay in people's minds with one very big asterisk next to it.

Ronaldo and his Internazionale went into the match, the fourth from last, just one point behind *La Signora*. A victory would have put them two points ahead; a draw would have kept them in striking range. Instead, Juventus, with the help of referee Piero Ceccarini of Livorno, virtually wrapped up the season. Ceccarini somehow failed to award a penalty against Mark Iuliano, a Juventus defender who played a split second of ice hockey in blocking Ronaldo. Iuliano, correctly sensing danger as Ronaldo had just touched the ball in the area, went for the man. He never even looked for the ball.

Unfortunately, Ceccarini let play proceed. While half of Inter's squad remained at that end of the pitch to protest, manager Gigi Simoni lost his temper and went on to the field. Play went on. Zinedine Zidane brought the ball down, and passed to Alessandro Del Piero in the area. Nigerian defender Taribo West shut down the threat, but not without fouling Del Piero. As if to add insult to injury, Ceccarini awarded a penalty shot to Juve. The *Interisti* were out of their minds, and pushed the ref back to the centre of the field. Simoni was ejected.

The only consolation of the day was that Inter's keeper, Gianluca Pagliuca, blocked Del Piero's penalty shot. But the damage was already done. Inter were denied their chance to draw with Juve, who were leading 1–0. That's how the game ended, but then the storm began.

It started with the softspoken Ronaldo. Inter were supposed to be in *silenzio stampa*, but what happened at Turin was too outrageous for the team to remain silent. 'How can you not call a penalty like that?' Ronaldo asked. 'Everyone saw it except the referee, and he was in position to see it. I feel like I've been robbed. I know I'll be fined, but it's impossible to remain silent.' Inter lost just about every chance they had for the *scudetto* in that moment, and Ronaldo let his feelings be known. 'During this season there have been a lot of questionable episodes, a lot of favours for the black and whites,' he said. 'At least in this match, which was so decisive, it shouldn't have happened. Football is joy, but only when you play eleven against eleven. It becomes sad when you play eleven against twelve, and the twelfth man is the ref.'

Marcello Lippi's Juventus have proven to be a stellar squad – Ancelotti always calls it the best in the world – but their directors didn't show nearly the class their players have after this key match. 'Ronaldo missed a good opportunity to keep quiet; he's learned Italian too quickly,' hissed director general Luciano Moggi. 'He should learn from Del Piero, who keeps his mouth shut and scores.'

Not exactly a class act, but Moggi, a former employee of the

Italian railways, has become one of the most powerful men in football. He has informants at other clubs and scouts throughout the country; if there's a 14-year-old with exceptional talent from a small town in Sicily, you can bet that Moggi knows about him. The president of the squad, Vittorio Caissotti di Chiusano, claimed it wasn't clear that Iuliano's collision with Ronaldo was a foul. Perhaps he should have looked at the replays and simply kept quiet. Juve's vice-president, Roberto Bettega, also fell into the trap of trying to say something cute: 'I don't know if we'll win the *scudetto*. In any case, I hope Inter don't have to wait another nine years before they win it again.'

Inter's owner, Massimo Moratti, left the stadium early. 'I don't like being made fun of,' Moratti said. 'The truth is that the refs are afraid of doing any harm to Juventus. I don't accuse Juve; it's a complex that the referees have.' The conflict went on for several days. Parliament was suspended briefly, and politicians, priests, players and just about anybody with an interest in the game discussed the incident. The Rome daily *Il Messaggero*, never very friendly to Juventus, called Juve's pivotal victory 'the Scudetto of Scandal'. *La Gazzetta dello Sport* printed a front-page editorial in which it praised the drive and determination of Lippi's squad, but concluded that there had been too many questionable decisions that had fallen for the white and blacks during the season. 'This won't go down in history as a clean championship,' the paper said.

Vatican Radio interviewed an 80-year-old cardinal, Fiorenzo Angelini, on the controversy. 'Even a one-eyed man with his good eye half closed would have seen that this was a penalty,' Angelini charged. 'It would have been better if the Juventus players at least recognized this, and that they got a break from the ref's error.' While the guilty party, Mark Iuliano, wouldn't admit his mistake, keeper Angelo Peruzzi very delicately did suggest that Juve won only with help on this occasion. 'Normally I have fun playing football,' Peruzzi said. 'Today I didn't.'

On the Wednesday after the game, Parliament dealt with the referee problem during 'question time' and that turned out to be almost as controversial as the match itself. A right-wing deputy and anti-*Juventino*, Domenico Gramazio, insulted a left-wing deputy, and ex-Juve player, Massimo Mauro. Gramazio loudly accused Juventus of having bought the refs, while Mauro called him a fool. The situation in Parliament came a lot closer to getting violent than the match itself did, and there would have been a good fistfight had ushers not kept the two men apart. Gramazio was suspended from Parliament for fifteen days and Mauro was censured.

But the polemics didn't end there. The man responsible for assigning the various referees to the different matches, Fabio Baldas, finally spoke about the incident. Baldas was at the match at Torino. 'In television, the episode is a lot more striking than when you see it from the stands,' Baldas said. 'Seen on TV, the foul on Ronaldo was as big as a house. I was at the stadium and I didn't have a perfect grasp of the foul. This year the referees haven't been any worse than past years, but I'm dismayed by the nastiness with which people are going after us.'

No, perhaps the refs weren't any worse than in previous years. They just happened to have made their biggest mistakes in a few terribly important games, yet no 'instant replay' or any other significant changes were in the works. However, when the Italian Football Federation met in July, it did decide that referees for Serie A and B matches the following season would be chosen by lottery, and not by an official designator.

18 May, or How Ancelotti Almost Got His Job Back

Millions of Italians play a guessing game every week during the season. *Totocalcio* is a kind of legalized betting in which you try to determine the results — win, lose or draw — of thirteen different professional matches. 'To do thirteen' in Italian has come to mean having extraordinary luck in any field at all. Ancelotti admits that he's no good at *Totocalcio*, and doesn't play. Parma's Mister simply isn't capable of looking at the match-ups coldly; he has to go with his heart, which doesn't help much for nailing down the right combinations: 'I always want Milan, Roma and Parma to win.'

He's particularly misty-eyed about Milan. 'You don't have to worry about anything there except playing football,' Ancelotti recalls, wistfully. 'I remember when I first went there. They found a nice house for us and then took my wife to a decorator's shop to choose furniture and all the rest. They told her, "All we want is that you be happy when you leave here." Well, she was happy all right. She cleaned the place out.'

Ancelotti doesn't hide the fact that Milan would be his 'dream job' as a coach. Roma is a close second, for the city and the squad, but his best memories are those from the north. Right now it's simply a dream, although when Milan went into a major crisis for the second time this season, Ancelotti's name came up as a possible successor. Fired from Parma and hired by Milan. That would certainly be 'doing thirteen'.

Strange as it may sound, it wasn't entirely out of the question. After Milan foolishly let the Italian Cup Final slip away on April 29, Fabio Capello's job suddenly looked like it was on the line, and two days later papers reported that Ancelotti would be a possible candidate. His name was on the front page of *La Gazzetta dello Sport*, and *La Repubblica* also mentioned him. He may look like a farm boy, but twenty years in the big leagues have taught Ancelotti a bit of media savvy. 'It's not important whether these things are true or not,' Parma's Mister suggested, with a grin. 'What's important is that they keep talking about you.'

And *La Repubblica* profiled Ancelotti in glowing terms. 'Milan would be an extraordinary temptation for Parma's good coach, who knows so well all of the thorny problems at the club,' the paper said. 'It would be a choice of head and of heart to come back and to have fun and to win, words that are out of place and far away here today.' While Milan was in crisis, Ancelotti had engineered a mini-comeback for Parma. The squad seemed to have regained their motivation. They were out of all the Cups and had lost all hope for the *scudetto*, but they still had to make UEFA and, perhaps more importantly, show their Mister they hadn't given up. For three games they played with the will to win, and chalked up victories over Naples at home, and Lecce and Lazio away, before they let Sampdoria get away with a draw at Parma on May 3.

But the one point from that draw assured Parma of a place in the UEFA Cup. Something of the season had been salvaged, although the Mister continued to have serious regrets. He didn't want to mention names, but he felt that he had been let down by the entire team. 'No one played better than expected,' Ancelotti concluded. 'And a lot of them went through the season well below what we were hoping from them.' Chiesa scored a goal against Sampdoria but he should have scored two or three. Parma's 'bomber' was more like a dud; with two games left he had scored only 10 goals in Serie A matches, not even half of what Bierhoff, Ronaldo and Del Piero had accomplished.

And yet Ancelotti had not lost faith in Enrico Chiesa. If he could choose any two strikers in A, he claims he'd take Chiesa and Ronaldo. 'It would be a killer cocktail of speed, skill and show,' Ancelotti said.

★   ★   ★

The worst ten minutes of Fabio Capello's life as a manager took place on the evening of April 29; swiftly followed by the worst five days. Capello's Milan went into the Final of the Italian Cup at Lazio with a 1–0 victory from the first leg. All they needed in Rome was a 0–0 or 1–1 draw and the Cup would be theirs. After a scoreless first half, Demetrio Albertini widened the Devils' aggregate score to 2–0 with a free-kick. But then everything fell apart.

Milan, who had bought and sold 27 players in the past three years, and boast three Italian national team starters (Albertini in midfield, Paolo Maldini and Alessandro Costacurta in defence), disappeared. Lazio, who now needed three goals to win, got them, as Milan's supposed Supermen, guys like George Weah, Ibrahim Ba and Marcel Desailly, committed a kind of collective suicide. Lazio scored one goal immediately, and then got a favourable decision for a penalty kick. The third one they earned, and that was that. The only thing 10th-placed Milan had left to salvage in a disastrous season was the Italian Cup, and they blew a 2–0 lead to lose even that consolation prize.

To make matters worse, they played the Final in front of their owner, Silvio Berlusconi, who was furious. Like most rich people who have spent millions of dollars trying to develop a squad, Berlusconi loves winning, and loves winning big, but hates losing, and really hates losing stupidly. 'We looked for the loss and we found it,' Berlusconi said, bitterly. And then, in a pointed accusation at his manager, and the would-be saviour of Milan, he added, 'I've never seen a team that's ahead by two goals pull one of its strikers.'

But Milan not only gave away the Final of the Italian Cup, they also continued to falter in Serie A. On May 3 in Rome, just four days after the humiliating Cup loss with Lazio, Milan fell 5–0 to Roma. Was there to be no end to the freefall? Milan had been sure that their 11th-place finish in the 1996–97 season was simply a bad memory from the past after they brought Capello back from Real Madrid. But this was not to be the case. With two games left, once-magical Milan sat ten places down from Juve, and were going nowhere fast.

'I ask forgiveness from our fans, and from Doctor Berlusconi,' Capello said after losing 5–0 with Roma. 'I'm ashamed of what I saw today. Sorry, but I'm not answering any questions. Thanks.' Berlusconi was certainly going to have some questions for his manager, and the national team skipper, Cesare Maldini, might also have had some questions – for himself – after seeing Milan disintegrate. Two of Milan's four defenders were starters on the Italian national team. Could he afford to take that kind of defence to Paris? His son Paolo, and Costacurta, never looked worse.

'I know that they've been criticized,' Maldini Sr. said. 'But I don't think they're in crisis. They've had a good season, and that can't be cancelled by a couple of bad games. A little crisis is normal for everyone. You can't always be at your top. Now's not the time for a revolution, and calling up just anyone. This championship hasn't shown any great stars except for the usual ones, and I know the usual ones.'

Milan's woes were evident in the dissension among their would-be champions. Liberian striker George Weah made no effort to hide his disappointment with his team-mates after the loss to Lazio in the Italian Cup. 'I'm angry because there are players here who don't give a damn about Milan,' Weah said. 'Capello can talk but he can't play. We are the ones who play and we're the ones who make mistakes. The other night a lot of people cried, and I cried too, but not only because Milan lost a game. I cried for us, because here there are so many people who didn't do what they should have done. There's not a sense of responsibility here. We, the players, made a mistake. All of us, myself included, obviously.'

Weah didn't want to hear talk about the 'old spirit' of Milan, once the strongest team in Europe. 'A team's a team,' Weah said. 'I don't know what the old spirit was, and why first we used to win with these players, and now we don't win any longer. What happened in these two years is difficult to explain.'

Ancelotti, the former *Milanista*, would agree. 'It's hard to create harmony in a team, especially when you have three managers over the course of two seasons,' he said. 'Then they exaggerated a bit in buying players, a great number of foreigners with different cultures: Brazilians, Dutch, French, Swedes, Slavs, etc. Undoubtedly this wasn't conducive to creating a compact group.'

At the beginning of the season, all the 'experts' had Milan among the top squads. Ancelotti himself had thought they would finish 3rd. 'This is proof once again that in football one good player plus another good player don't make a winning squad,' he said. 'Sure, it's absolutely, necessary to have strong players, but it's not the individual that counts.'

With three games left in the season, Inter trailed Juventus by four points. With three points for a victory, that was not an insurmountable lead. But Inter blew their chances on May 3, when they only managed a draw with Piacenza, 14th in the rankings. Juve tied the same day with Vicenza, and an Inter victory would have closed the gap to two points. But it wasn't on the cards. Inter hit the post twice and Piacenza's keeper, Matteo Sereni, played the game of his life, with a half dozen decisive saves. The young Nigerian Kanu missed an easy goal and the referee failed to call a hand ball against Piacenza in the penalty area. Internazionale dominated against the only all-Italian squad in Serie A. Inter landed 12 shots on goal to Piacenza's 2, but walked away dejectedly with their first 0–0 draw of the season.

Ronaldo's two-game disqualification for his comments after Juve–Inter had been nullified in what was a curious case of football justice. It didn't really make up for the penalty shot he never got to take against Juve. But not even the Phenomenon could tame Piacenza and keep the blue and blacks in the running, even though one of the unlucky post shots was his. Juventus took one more big step towards winning their 25th *scudetto*.

'The Lady' won the championship the following week. She came from behind against Bologna to beat Roberto Baggio and company 3–2. It was Filippo Inzaghi's day, as he scored all three goals. Juve locked up the Serie A title a week early, and all they had to worry about was the Champions League Final on May 20 in Amsterdam against Real Madrid. Inter faltered again, losing

174

2–1 to Bari, who were ecstatic because they were sure to remain in Serie A.

If May 10 marked Juve's new reign as Italian champions, the same date meant D-Day for Milan manager Fabio Capello. Milan played at home against Parma, but the Devils' fans disrupted the entire afternoon. The team had trouble getting into the ground as fans lay down in front of the gate in which the squad's bus enters. The bus backed up, accompanied by the jeers and gestures of their angry supporters. Inside San Siro, it wasn't much better. The upper decks were covered with banners in which the fans attacked their players for the disastrous season. One was especially harsh: 'Incompetence + Arrogance, Capello Go Home.'

The supporters-turned-antagonists had the entire afternoon planned out. They whistled loudly as each of the Milan players was announced before the game, and cheered for Ancelotti as his name came over the loudspeaker. Milan played poorly, as they had for much of the season, and the reaction from the fans certainly didn't help. At one point they got the entire stadium to turn their backs to the pitch in disgust. Parma scored in the first half when Faustino Asprilla, making a rare start, crossed to Crippa, who blasted a shot from the edge of the penalty area by the keeper. In one more public show of loyalty, Crippa ran immediately to the Parma bench and gave Ancelotti a big embrace.

It wasn't much of a game, and neither team played very well. Enrico Chiesa missed a chance to put the match away for Parma, and Milan evenutally drew even with a George Weah header. But the sideshow had become the main event, and the fans abandoned the upper deck at one point, leaving a long banner reading, 'Remain Alone with Your Shame.' Actually, they just moved to the lower deck, where they began pelting the pitch with oranges, eggs and water bottles. The referee kept appealing to Milan captain Alessandro Costacurta to do something, but the long-time defender simply kept his head down, looking at his shoes. He might as well have been in shock.

The game was delayed for seven minutes, and even when it was over, the show still wasn't over. The *tifosi* waited outside the gates for the players to come out and heaped abuse on them. Some players left in taxis rather than their own cars, thinking it would be safer. In a news conference after the match, Capello said he understood the anger of the *Milanisti* and that he accepted their antics. 'When you make a mistake you have to expect a reaction like that,' he said. 'We accept it.'

Ancelotti appeared to be in good spirits after the game. Although he prefers to wear a tracksuit to matches, this time he came in a blue suit. When one of the reporters pointed that out, suggesting that it was more in the 'Milan style', Ancelotti laughed: 'I notice that you're very attentive.' But Carletto's dream of managing Milan would have to wait. Although his name was on the short list of candidates, the favourite was Alberto Zaccheroni of Udinese. Milan had just bought from Udinese the season's top scorer, Oliver Bierhoff, and they were also in negotiations for Danish midfielder Thomas Helveg. 'Zac', a hot property at the moment, would go along with them, and Ancelotti would go home.

19 The Shake-Up

Stefano Tanzi met with Ancelotti on the Thursday night before the final game of the season, which was played on Saturday instead of Sunday. Young Tanzi made it official for the Mister; the experiment was over, and Parma were hiring Alberto Malesani. Tanzi explained that the Parma directors wanted to turn a new page for the club. Tanzi talked of the need for a 'big shake-up'.

It was a difficult meeting for Ancelotti. Although the Mister is not even ten years older than the president of the club, he was already playing in Serie A before Stefano had begun high school. 'I told him I didn't understand why they were doing this, and that I thought the entire affair had been handled quite badly,' Ancelotti recalled. 'It did a lot of harm to the team, and really got me quite angry. If they had told me earlier that it was over, I would have paid a lot more attention to other possibilities.'

Despite the unpleasant air, Ancelotti had been preparing for that meeting for a couple of months, and wasn't particularly shaken. He could now start looking seriously at other offers, although admittedly, in May, it was already late in the day. All the big boys have already lined up their dance partners. He got a call from the Turkish club Fenerbahçe of Istanbul, who made him an extremely lucrative offer, but he turned them down. The Spanish club, Zaragoza, also came after him, but Carletto wanted to stay put, at least for a while. His kids were happy living in Parma, and that was reason enough to remain in Emilia-Romagna.

Then Fenerbahçe upped their ante, almost making it an offer he couldn't refuse. Since he still had a contract with Parma Calcio, Ancelotti would make about £500,000 by staying at home, just as his buddy Sacchi had done for a year before he got the mega-offer from Atlético Madrid. But the Turks wanted to give him more than £1 million for a year's work. Four men from the club came to see him on Saturday, May 16, to try to convince him to go to Istanbul. The Mister was tempted but wanted to think about it for a week. Not that he needed the money, but the financial package was appealing. In addition, Fenerbahçe had finished 2nd in the Turkish league, and would be competing in the Champions League.

The money was a plus, as was the fact that the job would keep Ancelotti employed. There was a disadvantage in being out of Italy. Carlo thought that if he were to leave the country, it would be better to go to a powerful team in England, Spain or France, where his visibility would remain high. But he was almost willing to take a chance in Istanbul, as was his wife Luisa. Young Davide was game as well, but Katia didn't want to leave all her friends in Parma.

A week after Carlo was fired, his wife ran across Calisto Tanzi in a physiotherapist's office in Parma. She could have simply let him pass with a polite but impersonal exchange – 'Buon giorno, buon giorno', since it wasn't the moment for one of those 'So how are the kids?' conversations. But Luisa is more than the manager's wife. She's also his agent, and she wanted an answer about Carlo's sacking. Tanzi Sr laid the responsibility for the decision on his 30-year-old son, telling her that it was 'very difficult'. Luisa didn't find the answer satisfactory, and told Tanzi to his face she thought he was playing Pontius Pilate.

Unfortunately, the squad let Ancelotti down in the last game of the season, against 15th-place Brescia. The loss was almost to have been expected. Ancelotti has often toyed with using a theme song from one of the *Rocky* films, 'Eye of the Tiger', to get his boys psyched up for a match, but at his last Serie A match with Parma the song that was going through his mind was 'Killing Me Softly'.

Faustino Asprilla started again and showed a little spark, but couldn't make the difference. Although Dino Baggio put Parma ahead 5 minutes into the game, the defence didn't hold up and

Brescia, who were on their way to Serie B, scored three goals. It wasn't exactly a glorious goodbye for Carletto.

Parma had already made the UEFA Cup, and had no real incentive in the match. A win would have given them 4th place, behind Juventus, Internazionale, and Udinese; instead they ended up in 6th, behind Fiorentina on goals scored, as Roma jumped into 4th place with a victory over Sampdoria.

Fiorentina, as usual, ended the season with a curious internal battle. Gabriel Batistuta wanted to leave the club – possibly to go with Malesani to Parma – but still had time left on his contract, and Cecchi Gori wasn't budging. Fiorentina's owner hung his own banner at the team's last game, just to make it clear: 'Batistuta's Not For Sale–The President.' It wasn't clear whether Cecchi Gori, who had brought in veteran coach Giovanni Trapattoni as manager, was serious about keeping Batistuta, or simply wanted to raise the price. Batistuta had scored 21 goals throughout the season, none of them from penalty kicks (which Fiorentina no longer let him take after he missed three in a row).

The season ended with no surprises, although Oliver Bierhoff and Ronaldo each scored two goals in the final game; the German forward won the top scorer's award with 27, and the Brazilian followed with 25. Roberto Baggio also scored a couple, to bring his season's tally to 22, sparking more cries for Cesare Maldini to take him to France for the World Cup. Those cries would be heard. And when Alessandro Del Piero came away from the Champions League Final injured, Baggio had a chance of a starting position with the Azzurri. 'Little Buddha' was well sponsored, and Paolo Rossi, Italy's top scorer in the 1982 Cup, declared that Baggio should be starting alongside Christian Vieri in attack. 'He's got a lot of experience, so the emotional impact of a World Cup won't be a problem,' Rossi said. 'Technically speaking, his agility would be the perfect complement to Christian's power.'

Enrico Chiesa had a mediocre year at Parma and was initially excluded from the squad, but Maldini later called for him just in case Del Piero didn't heal. Zola had to take consolation in his goal in Chelsea's Cup victory, since there was apparently no room on the national team for the little Sardinian. His goal that gave Italy a victory over England at Wembley seemed to have been forgotten.

Lazio lost again in their final match, and fell into 7th place. The Eagles rose like a rocket mid-season and fell like a rock at the end, managing only to win the Italian Cup. In the *campionato*, they dropped below Parma, Fiorentina, and dreaded rival Roma. After the final games, the 34th match of the season, the table looked like this:

Juventus	74
Inter	69
Udinese	64
Roma	59
Fiorentina	57
Parma	57
Lazio	56
Bologna	48
Sampdoria	48
Milan	44
Bari	38
Empoli	37
Piacenza	37
Vicenza	36
- - - - - - - - - - - -	
Brescia	35
Atalanta	32
Lecce	26
Napoli	14

Despite their lifeless stadium, Juventus were unbeatable at home. In 17 matches in Turin, they won 15 and tied 2. Playing away, they had 6 victories, 9 draws and 2 losses.

Inter lost 2 at San Siro and 5 away.

Ancelotti remained with Parma throughout the month of May, as they played a series of friendlies in Spain. The post-season would normally allow a manager to take a look at his youngsters, and call up a few kids from the junior team, but Ancelotti didn't really care any longer. When the time came to go on 'retreat' in the mountains in July to prepare for the following season, he wouldn't be the manager.

He was angry, above all with Parma, but also with himself. 'I made some mistakes,' he said. 'Mostly in evaluating our team. I looked at our splendid '96–97 season, and was sure that we could repeat it with the guys we had. Unfortunately, that's not the way it worked out.'

Despite what the papers had written, managing Milan was never a serious possibility. The Mister recounted: 'They told me that they were looking for someone who wasn't too "friendly" with the players.' Ancelotti's links with Milan remain quite strong, and Berlusconi's squad needed new blood. The argument was similar to the one Tanzi Jr. used with Ancelotti, that it was time for a big shake-up. In the meantime, in addition to Zaragoza and Fenerbahçe, two other teams came knocking at Carlo's door, AIK Athens and Stuttgart.

But if Carlo turned down more than a million pounds for a year in Istanbul, he wasn't going to take off for Greece or Germany either. 'The motives are mainly the family, since it's just not the right thing at this moment,' he reasoned. 'And since I don't plan for managing too long, better to do it in Italy than elsewhere.' He figures he'll use the time to catch up on his football 'studies', taking a look at as many new players as he can.

The worst games of the season for Fabio Cannavaro remained crystal clear in his mind: Sparta Praga knocking in a goal at the last minute to put Parma out of the Champions League, and Patrick Kluivert's goal in the final second for Milan to end the *gialloblu*'s quest for the Italian Cup. 'We weren't as compact as we had been the previous year,' Cannavaro said. 'We weren't mean or aggressive. The year before we'd fight until the final whistle, until death. This season we were too naïve.'

It's difficult, or at least mistaken, to be overconfident in Serie A, where any squad can defeat you on a given Sunday, but Cannavaro believes that's what happened to Parma. 'We were too sure of ourselves, convinced we had this stupendous defence,' he said. 'That kind of thinking leads you to a lack of concentration.' There were also other factors that hindered the effectiveness of the once-mighty defence this season, and Cannavaro pointed out that they conceded 13 goals from free-kicks, as opposed to only 4 the previous year. 'That's not only the problem of the backs,' said Cannavaro, adding that the defence was 'not as well protected' by the midfield as it had been the year before.

Parma's poster-boy refused to lay the blame on the Mister. Although he's one player who likes to clown around with the others, he's also one of the few who refers to Ancelotti with the formal '*lei*' instead of the familiar '*tu*'. Cannavaro grew up in the south, in Naples, where respect for your elders and superiors still means something. 'It was a problem of players, not the manager,' Cannavaro said. 'The fact that a number of players had a bad year is what produced a bad season for us.'

Cannavaro did offer mild criticism of his friend Ancelotti, however. 'He probably had too much faith in thirteen or fourteen players and could have substituted more,' he said. 'He wasn't very flexible in this, but at the same time you have to admit that he didn't have all that many alternatives this year.'

Although he's only 24, Cannavaro has already seen half a dozen Serie A managers, given that his former squad, Napoli, used to change them nearly every season. He remains especially impressed with Marcello Lippi, the brains of Juventus, for his ability to 'read' a game. 'As he watches the match he knows how to change the positioning or change the players to find the right solution,' he said. 'That's his strength.'

Having come from Napoli, Cannavaro recognizes better than most players the need for long-range planning, and the disasters that can come when it's missing. He had no qualms about saying he was 'absolutely against' the Mister's ousting at Parma. 'There's no way I would have changed managers,' he said. 'In the Mister's first season we made it to the Champions League, and this year we're in UEFA. Sure, we didn't achieve the objectives we wanted, but it seems a bit much to get rid of him.'

Cannavaro believes firing the manager is the 'easy solution' to a team's troubles. 'It's a lot easier to change managers than to change the team or the directors,' he said. 'An important team needs a very good *direttore sportivo* [head of player personnel], and Parma don't have one.' Cannavaro has never met Malesani, but his friends at Fiorentina tell him that Parma's new Mister is a decent guy. 'They spoke very well of him,' Cannavaro said. 'From what I understand, he's a lot like Ancelotti.'

Epilogue

On June 10 I had to go to Bologna to interview pop singer Andrea Bocelli, and took advantage of the trip to see Ancelotti at home. It was the opening day of the World Cup, and he picked me up at the train station at half-time of the Brazil–Scotland match. He was already on vacation, dressed in shorts, sandals and a tennis shirt. We went home and watched the second half with his wife Luisa. She had bet on Brazil and wanted them to win; I rooted against them since they had beaten Italy four years before. Ancelotti didn't seem to care who won, but was tremendously impressed by the individual skills of the Latin Americans, especially Cafu and Denilson.

After the match, while Luisa played tennis with a friend, Carlo and I went on to the porch and talked about the season. I had been aware that Luisa wanted to go to Istanbul and purposely avoided that subject when we were all together. 'Yeah, better not to talk about it,' Carlo said. 'She still thinks we should have gone.' Luisa loves exotic places. The Ancelotti home, which is the house Luisa grew up in as a child, is curiously devoid of any reference to football. No shirts, no trophies, no pennants. Instead, it's filled with the oriental art that Luisa has collected.

Carlo criticized his own coaching on two points, and they were related. 'We came in 2nd place the previous season, and I had too much confidence in the roster as it was,' he said. 'I was sure that we could repeat a great season. I should have insisted that we buy some more players. That would have created some competition for the starting jobs, and the quality would have been better.' Ironically, when Malesani came in, Parma went on a shopping spree, and only lavish Lazio dished out more than they did on new players.

Carlo's son, Davide, was on vacation in Sardinia with his grand-mother, and called punctually at 8 p.m., just like he was supposed to. Katia was home and had a friend visiting, and pleaded with Dad to let her spend the night at her schoolmate's house. She succeeded.

We had pizza and beer for dinner, and strawberries for dessert. Carlo sometimes let Katia play secretary for him, answering his cell phone and telling the callers that he was busy. After dinner Carlo called Mario Stanic, who was playing in the Cup for Croatia, to wish him good luck. (Croatia proved to be the biggest surprise of the World Cup, blanking Germany 3–0 to make it to the semi-finals, and Ancelotti's friend 'Big Mario' ran a tough and aggressive midfield along with another Serie A player, Milan's Zvonimir Boban. The normally serious Stanic showed some flair when he bleached his hair at the Cup.) We then went back into the living room to watch Norway–Morocco. Ancelotti had difficulty understanding Norway's kick-and-run football. 'Get ready for BOOM!' he said, as a Norwegian defender set up to kick the ball 60 metres downfield. 'I don't know what that is, but it's not football.'

Ancelotti would be heading to France in a few days to do some commentary on one of the RAI's World Cup shows. He looked forward to seeing as much football as he could, both in the World Cup and next season, 'studying up' on teams and players. He'll probably want to go see his friend Arrigo Sacchi's Atlético Madrid, but he said he won't set foot again in the Parma grounds. 'It wouldn't be right,' he said.

The World Cup quarter-final stage pitted Italy against France, but it looked a lot like a Sunday afternoon game in Milan or Turin, with so many players from Milan, Inter and Juventus on the field – such is the strength of Serie A. The French midfield came courtesy of Juventus, with Didier Deschamps and Zinedine Zidane, the eventual hero of the tournament, along with Inter's Youri Djorkaeff, while Marcel Desailly of Milan anchored the defence. Also in defence, of course, but playing wing-back instead of centre-back, was Parma's Lilian Thuram, who brought France back from the brink of disaster in the semi-finals against Croatia.

Two other French players on the bench, Vincent Candela and Alain Boghossian, spent the season in Italy (at Roma and Sampdoria respectively) and an additional four had previously played on Italian squads. All told, there were 53 players from Serie A on the eight teams that made it to the quarter-finals, more than twice the number from the runner-up, Germany's Bundesliga. AC Milan alone had 12 representatives on national teams in the quarter-finals.

Deschamps and Zidane found themselves up against their Juventus team-mates Alessandro Del Piero and Gianluca Pessotto, who had the tough task of marking Zidane, the French playmaker. 'If France wins, it's thanks to you guys,' Zidane joked before the match, and there was some truth to what he said. Youri Djorkaeff did his best in trying to score against his friend at Inter, Italian keeper Gianluca Pagliuca (and he nearly did in the second period of extra-time), while Fabio Cannavaro exchanged words with Thuram, his fellow defender at Parma, after a collision near the Italian goal.

'This is a match that's worthy of the Final,' Pagliuca said before kick-off. 'It's too bad we have to play it now.' That was true. It may not have been beautiful, but it was terribly combative. In the end, France outplayed Italy but couldn't score during 90 minutes of regulation or 30 minutes of sudden-death extra-time, despite several good chances. *Les Bleus* won only on penalty kicks, 4–3. However, they dominated most of the game, and deserved the victory, forcing twelve corner kicks to Italy's three. Italy nearly sneaked by with a 'golden goal' in extra-time, but Roberto Baggio's volley went just wide.

In the days prior to the match, all the attention was on Zidane, who powered Juventus to the *scudetto* and serves as field commander for France as well. Zidane came back against Italy after a two-game suspension, and was well rested, although Pessotto kept him under control for most of the match. 'He's a midfield Ronaldo,' Dino Baggio said of Zizou, and apparently believed it. Baggio, a tough defensive player, told Cesare Maldini he'd rather not have the task of marking Zidane, and the Mister gave the job to Pessotto.

Michel Platini, organizer of France '98, made no bones about his love for Italian football. 'Juventus is what made me known around the world,' he said. 'I spent five marvellous years there and we won everything.' Platini was known as 'King Michel' in Italy, and Giovanni Agnelli, whose family owns Juventus, considers him the best of all time. Agnelli, who watched the game with Henry Kissinger, was amused by the intensity of the build-up. 'The French think they're superior to us, and if something happens to the contrary, they're really bothered by it.'

The French were superior, but not by much. They were certainly better in midfield, and perhaps in defence as well, although their attack was appallingly weak. They only got by Croatia when, after going down 1–0, Lilian Thuram took the game into his own hands and scored twice. Ironically, Thuram had not scored a goal all season with Parma, although he had come close to heading in a few corner kicks, and got robbed once by Lazio's keeper on a breakaway. 'With those feet of his I don't know how he ever put the ball in the net,' joked Cannavaro after the match.

The first person Thuram called after the biggest match of his life was Ancelotti. Parma's former coach had always insisted that Thuram was one of the best in football today, and the defender's performance in the World Cup was proof of that. If the French strikers couldn't score, that wasn't his fault. Although Zidane became the hero of the Final with two goals in France's 3–0 victory over Brazil, there was no excuse for his stomping a player in the first match, and Thuram and Didier Deschamps proved to be more valuable over the course of seven games. French captain Deschamps played flawlessly in midfield, but it was Thuram, the softspoken jazz lover – he's a big fan of Miles Davis – who was the game-maker, the *trascinatore*. At Parma he had occasionally shown signs of imperiousness; in France he was both imperious and impetuous. Although he played most spectacularly against Croatia, the French would have never made it to the semi-finals had Thuram not shut down Alessandro Del Piero and the French defence only allowed the Italians one decent scoring chance in extra-time of the quarter-final.

France risked losing to Paraguay, and Zidane's sitting out probably had something to do with that. Desailly also got sent off for a stupid foul in the Final, and France were forced to play with ten men for the last quarter of the game. Desailly played far better for France than he had for Milan during the regular season, but credited his Italian colleagues for the success of *Les Bleus*. 'France has always produced good players but if we have a great national team today, it's because we've finally learned how to play together,' he said. 'And a lot of us have learned that in Italy.'

Italy's quest for the Cup began modestly, with a 2–2 draw against Chile. Fabio Cannavaro looked like he was a head too short as he tried to defend against Marcelo Salas, author of both Chilean goals. Roberto Baggio proved that, ageing or not, he was primed for these games. He delivered a splendid assist to Christian Vieri for the first goal of the game, and then hit a good penalty when Italy got a lucky decision towards the end of the game. Baggio would go on to score another pretty goal in the tournament, but Vieri was the powerhouse with five goals in five games, and may well have won the Golden Boot had Italy made it any further.

Dino Baggio didn't have a great game against France, and Maldini pulled him off, but otherwise he played solid football in the Cup. Cannavaro redeemed himself against the French, with a heroic and flawless performance, which became all the more impressive after he took a wicked elbow to the face from Stephane Guivarc'h. The *Gazzetta dello Sport* called him the best on the field. Cannavaro got to join Parma a week late on their mountain retreat because of the World Cup, and was enjoying himself on vacation in Naples in mid-July. 'The Cup was tough,' he said. 'The first game, I didn't play badly, but my man [Salas] scored twice. Then against France I played a great game but we lost.' His wife Daniela, who always prepares his notes and cards to sign for fans who write to him, has been busier than ever.

Enrico Chiesa got to play a little in the first match against Chile and then watched the rest of the games from the bench. Gianluigi Buffon, who become the number-two keeper after Peruzzi was injured, saw all of the Cup from the bench, as the veteran Gianluca Pagliuca manned the nets. Buffon will have to wait another four years to play in a World Cup, and Italy will probably need 'Superman' then. He's gained the reputation as a penalty-kick specialist, and the Azzurri have now been ousted three times on penalties. They can't seem to shoot them and they can't seem to stop them.

With a couple of big exceptions, the stars of Serie A kept shining in the World Cup. Alessandro Del Piero never pulled himself together for Italy and went home with no goals to his credit. Ronaldo played steadily if not spectacularly until the Final, when he disappeared after mysterious convulsions just hours before the game. Inter's owner Massimo Moratti was livid that Brazil put the Phenomenon in the game, and told his star, who had played 81 games in the course of the year, to take as much vacation as he wanted. Hernán Crespo didn't manage to show much stuff when he came in for Gabriel Batistuta in the Argentina–England match, and he blotted his book further when the match went to penalty kicks and he botched his.

Batistuta knocked in five goals for Argentina, while Ronaldo and the new *Laziale*, Chilean Marcelo Salas, each had four. Oliver Bierhoff (now with Milan) scored three for Germany, and provided a beautiful assist for his companion Jurgen Klinsmann, who also had three.

By midsummer Parma had picked up Abel Balbo, the Italo-Argentinian striker who was at Roma. New Mister Alberto Malesani tried desparately to bring Batistuta with him, but Cecchi Gori held firm. Parma did the same thing with Chiesa, who wanted to go to Milan. Parma did manage to pick up Juan Sebastian Veron from Sampdoria, along with another midfielder, Diego Fuser of Lazio. Alain Boghossian was also on his way to Parma, from Sampdoria, as was Inter's wing-back Luigi Sartor. Pedros, who had gone to Napoli and then Lyon on loan, was back because he had a four-year contract with the club, although Parma would try to offload him.

Parma lent Adailton to Paris Saint-Germain, and Strada and Zé Maria to Perugia, who had made it into Serie A. Blomqvist was headed to Manchester United, and there were negotiations to send Crippa to Torino (still stuck in B) and Sensini to Sampdoria. Parma directors were also looking for a place for Orlandini and Giunti.

In the meantime, Parma's coach before Ancelotti, Nevio Scala, left Borussia Dortmund and almost signed with Real Madrid, but the deal fell through at the last minute. Ancelotti took a long vacation in Sardinia with his family, watched the World Cup matches, and closed his contract with Parma. While he could have sat idle for two years and collected his paycheques, he negotiated with the squad to have part of the salary but to be free from all obligations. As happens every season in Serie A, jobs at big clubs will be opening up, and Ancelotti won't be far from his phone. 'I'm still in the market,' Carlo said. 'And I'd like to be coaching again soon.'